ABOUT THE BOOK

A Dialogue transcribed in AD 1385 in Tuscany, Italy has stimulated an interest returning a society under the guidance of humanity's Creator. A society's belief in God benefited a similar society in strife during the14th and 15th centuries in Europe that were of a Theo-Sociologic etiology through His profound teachings. Multiple solutions from God the Father's spoken words through a formally uneducated Theo-Political Dominican lay person 640 years later is developed into a new Dialogue format. Saint Catherine of Siena is recognized as one of the most remarkable women of the Middle Ages. The Dialogue of the spoken word of God the Father through Catherine was transcribed by Raymond of Capua and other Dominicans, while she was engaged in mystical trances between 1378-1379. She died in 1380 at the age of thirty-three. There are four major treatises with ninety subsections. All are related to Divine Mercy and God's love for humanity, through Jesus Christ and the Holy Spirit, embodied in the Holy Trinity, for the salvation of souls. The author breaks down a difficult treatise's 86,000 words into 28,000 words of salient theological concepts obtained solely from the Dialogue into sentences and paragraphs. This easily readable format has not been utilized in any language to the author's knowledge. This Dialogue in God's own words was on target for a population in political turmoil in Europe, as well as a Holy Church in need of reform. Thus, a 14th century Dialogue relevant in the 21st century.

GOD'S PEARLS

LOVE AND LIFE

SPOKEN THROUGH
SAINT CATHERINE OF SIENA

Transcribed by Raymond of Capua

Edited by:
RAY A HURM MD

14th Century Dialogue
Relevant in the 21st

Xulon Press Elite

Xulon Press Elite
2301 Lucien Way #415
Maitland, FL 32751
407.339.4217
www.xulonpress.com

Paperback ISBN-13: 978-1-6628-3079-2
Ebook ISBN-13: 978-1-6628-3080-8

DEDICATION

THE MOST HOLY TRINITY

GOD THE FATHER

GOD THE SON

GOD THE HOLY SPIRIT

STRING OF PEARLS: The rosary is a series of devotional prayers to Mary the Mother of God, as an intercession to Jesus Christ for the salvation of souls. It was introduced by Saint Dominic in the thirteenth century through a vision of the Blessed Virgin Mary. Variations have evolved over the ensuing centuries, but the rosary remains as a mainstay devotional in the Roman Catholic Church. Its significance was renewed in 1917 during apparitions in Portugal by Our Lady of Fatima and continues to the present day. Saint Catherine's prayer on the Feast of the Annunciation in 1378 (Drain 1882) continued, "Oh, Mary, I address myself to thee with boldness because I know that God cannot refuse thee."

TABLE OF CONTENTS

LIST OF ILLUSTRATIONS

TREE OF LOVE AND LIFE

The concept of a "Tree of Life" has been developed in various ways in prior literary works, but it is uniquely presented in the treatise of Discretion as a parable (II. #10). It has not been illustrated in any prior texts to the author's knowledge as developed.throughout Gods Pearls. Using the theme of this parable throughout the Dialogue's other three treatises expands the concept expressed as the "Tree of Love and Life" in Discretion by producing a cohesive illustrative theme throughout the four treatises.

PREFACE

Saint Catherine of Siena has been recognized as one of the most remarkable women of the Middle Ages. Needless to say, she was an individual chosen by God to change the history of the fourteenth and fifteenth centuries of Europe, along with the Roman Catholic Church. For readers who are not aware of her impact on history, the next section will provide a capsular insight of her life. The Dialogue with God the Father was transcribed by Blessed Raymond of Capua in 1385 (Cartier), along with other members of the Dominican order. The details of Saint Catherine's writings and veneration are not new to the Roman Catholic Church's history, legacy or theological documentation (Benedict XVI, 2011). Pope Paul VI designated Saint Catherine a doctor of the Roman Catholic Church in 1970 (catholicsaints.info/alphabetical-list, 2021).

The Dialogue, as a written treatise, was difficult for this novice author to understand confidently with its detailed passages after reading it for the first time. Then dissecting the treatise with an understanding of the fantastic applicability of a fourteenth century set of treatises to the twenty-first century. Next, the follow-up transition of salient concepts and quotations was developed in a coherent form that is presented in a new format. It was of the utmost importance to maintain quotations derived from one paragraph and tie quotations from another paragraph to produce conjoined statements from the same section of the treatise—in other words, producing understandable sentences and paragraphs.

The author's attempt to present an easier format to read than that of the original prosaic transcription may be viewed as an undesirable endeavor by some critics. The author tries to develop a more readable format so that a larger readership might be able to put into practice the important concepts presented in these works. There are changes in the use of pronouns throughout the treatises by substituting the words soul, person, humanity, one, and them for he, she, him and man, producing a lesser personal character to the verbiage between God in direct, one-on-one conversation with Catherine. This is done by the editor, developing a non-generic relationship with the concept that God's words to Catherine of Siena were personally intended for her; needless to say, but in retrospect, the Dialogue applies to all of humanity. This may seem like a stretch of a nuance of the Dialogue; however, one of the objects in the "Dialogue summary" states in God's words to Catherine:

"If thou rememberest well, thou didst make four petitions of Me with anxious desire, or rather caused thee to make them in order to increase the fire of My love in thy soul; one for thyself, which I have satisfied, illuminating thee with My truth, and showing thee how thou mayest know this truth which thou didst desire to know; explaining to thee how thou mightest come to the knowledge of it through the knowledge of thyself and Me, through the light of faith" (TAN Books, 2010, page 200).

The words thou, thee, and thy have also been exchanged for you, your and my, as well as the spelling of various verbs and adverbs. The four treatises present ninety sections that are distinctly different, but are all related to divine mercy and God's love for humanity by His only begotten Son, Jesus Christ, through the Holy Spirit, embodied in the Holy Trinity for the salvation of souls.

The Dialogue used by this author was personally obtained in the bookstore at the Basilica San Domenico in Siena, Italy. It is identical to the work of Algar Thorold, who used the Dialogue of Raymond of Capua's Latin documentation into the English in, "translating as literally as possible" (1896, ref.1). An original translation from French into English was developed by E.Cartier employing the Latin translation as its reference for accuracy for theological content (1860, ref. 3). It was originally documented in one volume, according to twentieth century researchers (Noffke 2002, Ferretti 2004). Historical accuracy of format is of secondary importance, compared to theological accuracy, in the opinion of this editor. The differences in the presentation of the theological concepts are in a more readable summary format. It splits each section into understandable theological concepts, sentence by sentence and quote by quote. This format, needless to say, completely changes the original Dialogue format, again in an attempt to expose its theological contents to a larger audience.

The four treatises present ninety sections that are distinctly different, but all are related to divine mercy and God's love for humanity through His only begotten Son, Jesus Christ with the Holy Spirit, embodied in the Holy Trinity for the salvation of souls (i. #6, II. #11, #20, #38, #48, III. #58, #72, #79). God's object of this dialogue for humanity is to "increase the fire of My love in your soul" (I. #4, II. #45, IV. #90).

Multiple, theological insights advancing salvation is developed in each of the ninety sections. From suffering in this earthly life (I. #3, #5, II. #35, III. #66) and Purgatory (I. #4, II. #33, #42, #55), both with their existence documented, as well the soul's disposition before the Final Judgement (II. #20, #30, #31, #32, #33). All are discussed along with the key to enter heaven (II. #18, #63, IV. #81 #82, #83). The reverence for priests, good or bad, is noted (III. #77) with the admonition for seculars to withhold judgement of errant priests (III. #78). Methods obtaining perfect love to be granted eternal salvation is explained in detail (I. #4, #77, II. #44, #45, #46, #47, #49, #51, #53, III. #64). Emphatic documentation is stated with reference to the Trinity (II. #20, #26, #46, III. #72) and Eucharistic Transubstantiation (III. #50, #58, #72, #73, #74). Hatred of anyone for any reason is discussed. "You will see remaining in hatred, you give Me by transgressing My precept...a deprivation of the life of grace" (IV, #83).

Living within the principles of this Dialogue will not only provide humanity with peace and happiness in this earthly life (III. #78), but it will give one the tools to obtain eternal life, which should be the goal of every human's faith in God, the Creator. Most importantly, the documentation of the human soul's components of memory, intellect and will producing a free will (II. #37) that is capable of choosing virtue or vice and consequently, arriving at eternal life (II. #38) or eternal death (II. #38, #79). This concept provides an understanding of conscience (III. #78) and a mechanism to develop a moral code, emanating from the love of God, who created the human race in His image and likeness with a soul (II. #37, III. #66). The "Law of Perversity" provides humanity the ability to develop a virtuous conscience through spiritual conflict by conquering perversity which is its sensual contrary (III. #66).

The first man and woman created with souls disobeyed the words of the Creator (I. #4, #6, II. #14,) to which their prodigy has dealt with the stain of that original sin ever since (II. #13, #33, IV. #81). One may ask," Why would an almighty, loving Creator do such a thing to humanity?" A greater, in-depth discussion will be developed in another book titled, *Tweeners*. Multiple treatises have evolved over the centuries trying to answer that question, and I'm sure a follow-up won't conclude the process of ontology. An attempt to better understand a biological etiology of a human conscience has been published by Norton & Company in New York, *Conscience, The Origins of Moral Intuition,* authored by Patricia S.Churchland, professor emerita of philosophy at the University of California, San Diego. It is eruditely written and magnificently researched with the title of the seventh chapter, "What does love have to do with It?" My answer is everything!!! Saint Catherine's Dialogue embellishes this answer (I. #1, II. #48, III. #49, #51, #52).

The author offers a definition of 'love' for humanity that is derived from this Dialogue as an infinite relationship between two or more entities, giving to the relationship that which is perceived as good for it by developing a certain conscience utilizing memory, intellect and free will consistent with the Creator's commands: first loving God, the Creator, above everything and second loving one's neighbor as one loves oneself unselfishly and unconditionally (II. #37. #38, #40). The challenge of trying to understand humanity's relationship with the Creator continues. God's love of humanity is a common theme of the entire Dialogue. Some of the specifically related sections are included in the following references; I. #1, II. #9, #13, #16, #44, #45, #46, III. #49, #51, # 58, #62, #66, #68, IV. #84, # 91.

The author's understanding of a human's soul through this Dialogue is that of a unique infinite entity created in the image and likeness of the Creator, composed of memory intellect and free-will, whose purpose is; first, to know, love serve, praise, honor and glorify God; second, develop a unitive state of the soul with God; third, through divine mercy to be with the Trinity for eternity (II. #10, #12, #31, #37, #38, #40, III. #54, #56, #58, #59, #62, #63, #66, #74).

The concept of a "Tree of Life" has been developed in various ways in prior literary works, but it is uniquely presented in the Treatise of Discretion as a parable (II. #10). It has not been illustrated in any prior texts to the author's knowledge as developed throughout *God's Pearls*. Using the theme of this parable throughout the Dialogue's other three treatises expand the concept expressed as the "Tree of Love and Life" in Discretion by producing a cohesive illustrative theme throughout the four treatises.

From this Dialogue one can develop a definition of a human being as a unique physical and infinite entity, the latter of which is composed of memory, intellect and free-will created in the image and likeness of the Creator, God the father, whose only begotten Son, Jesus Christ, and the Holy Spirit, all three of whom are united in a unique infinite relationship with each soul created to know, love, serve, praise, honor and glorify the Holy Trinity. The infinite power of God's love produces a unique relationship with humanity through an individual souls' ability to develop a certain conscience consistent with God's commands, "to love Me above everything and to love your neighbor as yourself." to be with the Triune God for eternal life.

SAINT CATHERINE OF SIENA'S LIFE

Many chronicles have documented the life of Catherine of Siena AD 1347-1380. An excellent bibliography from catholicsaints.info/alphabetical-list is noted in the references of this book. She was the twenty-fourth child of Lapa and Jocomo Benincasa of Siena, whose twin sister died in infancy. Catherine's mother knew that she was different than the rest of her twenty-four children and had a difficult time with her through early childhood and teenage life. At age seven, she had an apparition of Jesus, Peter, John, and Paul (E.Cartier, 1860). She became a Dominican tertiary at fifteen, working with the poor and sick. Her avocation taught her life's experiences, but without formal education. She did not learn to read or write until she was in her early twenties. Her natural beauty, sincere kindness, and leadership qualities provided her to be recognized within the Dominican Order, as well as the Roman Catholic hierarchy as a very special person (Drane, 1882). She was provided significant support, including secretaries to record advice that was requested of her not only by her Dominican sisters, but also by luminaries in Italian society. Officials in Rome and Pope Gregory XI realized that her talents were supernatural gifts. Mystical ecstasies, when recorded by her assistants, were understood by her confessors and Catholic prelates to be, "inspired by the Holy Spirit" (Drane, 1882). At least four hundred formal letters are archived as her special documents ranging from personal communications to official government correspondence. The latter category was accomplished when Saint Catherine became a principal envoy in returning the papacy to Rome from Avignon, France, in 1377, where it had been located for seventy years. She was held as a political hostage in northern Italy for several months, at the direction of the king of France, until all the political and church negotiations were finalized (Cartier, 1860). She then returned to Rome and Siena. Catherine, while in mystical trances, was in total communication with God and she verbalized His spoken word, through which the Dialogue was developed between 1378-1379 (Thorold, 1896). These events were witnessed and transcribed by her secretaries, as well as a "filial son," Stephen Maconi, and her Confessor Blessed Raymond of Capua, who eventually rose to the superior general of the Dominican order. The transcription of the Dialogue was carried out by Blessed Raymond of Capua translated from the Bollandista Italian dialect into Latin and completed in 1385 (Cartier, 1860). It was rewritten on official parchment, bound, and documented in the Roman Catholic Church archives in Avignon, France, and in Rome. (Cartier,1860). A bizarre situation developed after her death in 1380 when determining her entombment site, which was finally settled after three years, satisfying all involved parties (Cartier, 1860). Family, politicians and church prelates decided that her body would remain in the Dominican church of Santa Maria sopra Minivera in Rome. Her head would be removed and transported to Siena, where it remains to this day without significant corruption. Six hundred and forty years later, it can still be viewed in a special chapel in the Dominican church of Saint Dominic in the town of Siena, Italy. Saint Catherine was canonized in 1461 by Pope Pius II (Ferretti).

DIALOGUE

I. DIVINE PROVIDENCE
II. DISCRETION
III.PRAYER
IV.OBEDIENCE

I. DIVINE PROVIDENCE

#1. "To the soul who will love Me and will observe
My commandments, I will manefest Myself, and
that soul shall be one thing with Me and I with that soul."

TREE OF LOVE AND LIFE

HEAVEN

GRACE
VIRTUE
DISCRETION

↑

LOVE
HOLY SPIRIT

FRUIT
FLOWERS
BRANCHES

SOUL
(Infinite)
-Memory
-Intellect
-Free Will

The souls clear
vision of the
Divine Essence
of the
Eternal Trinity

✝

HEAVEN'S KEYS
are placed in the
hands of My Son
JESUS CHRIST
↑

TRUNK
(Finite)

SOIL
Soul's Humility

CREATOR
"The soul is created in My
image and likliness"

ROOT
God the Father

LOVE for humanity is an infinite relationship between
two or more entities, giving that which is perceived as good
for it by developing a certain conscience utilizing memory,
intellect and free will consistent with the Creator's commands:
first loving God, the Creator, above everything and second,
loving one's neighbor as one loves oneself unselfishly and
unconditionally. - R. A. HURM 2021

I. TREATISE OF DIVINE PROVIDENCE

Sections 1-8

1. UNION OF THE SOUL

"Jesus said, 'To the soul who will love Me and will observe My commandments I will manifest Myself and that soul shall be one thing with me and I with the soul.'"

2. GROWTH OF THE SOUL

"The neediness in the world is a tempest and offense against God...the loss of souls and the perspective of the Holy Church."

Prayer: "O Eternal Father, I accuse myself before You in order that You may punish me for my sins in this infidelity. As much as my sins are the cause of the sufferings which my neighbor must endure, I implore You in Your kindness to punish them in my person."

3. FINITE WORKS ACCOMPANIED BY LOVE

"I wish that you know that not all the pains that are given people in this life are given as punishments; some are corrections in order for the soul to develop true contrition, not through the pain endured but because I wish for infinite love and infinite sorrow."

"Sorrow for the soul's sins against Me, the soul's Creator, sorrow for which the soul sees its neighbor commit sins against Me."

"Saint Paul the Apostle's Quote:
'If I had tongues of angels, if I knew things of the future, I gave my body to be burned and do not have love, it would be worth nothing to me. Works must be produced in love... Finite works are not valid either as punishment or recompense."

4. SATISFACTION OF CONTRITION

"Desire and contrition of heart satisfy both guilt and the penalty in some and not in others. Sometimes it satisfies guilt, but not the penalty."

"Knowledge of one's own actions and thoughts generates a hatred and displeasure against sin and against the soul's own sensuality, through which the soul deems itself worthy of pain and unworthy of reward."

"Virtue cannot have life in itself except through charity and humility, the foster mother and nurse of charity."

"I have recreated you and washed you in the Blood of My only begotten Son, who spilt His Blood with so great a fire of love to teach you the truth. Self-knowledge is the only way you can learn to destroy the cloud of selfishness."

"If people arise with true patience and sorrow for their sins and love of virtue for the glory and praise of My Name, I will forgive humanity's sins through the virtue of love."

"To people who humbly and with reverence receive the doctrine of My servants, I will remit guilt and penalty by true knowledge and contrition of their sins by prayer and desire for serving Me through grace and their desires."

"Through love alone, I lead them back to grace so that My truth may be fulfilled in them."

"Since they are imperfect, they receive imperfectly the perfection of the desires of those who offer them to Me for their sakes."

"The devil has the right to seize on everything that humanity has acquired in this life through pride, selfishness, hatred, humiliation, and persecution of My servants. A person can obscure his or her intellect through a distorted will."

"If having abandoned mortal sin, a soul receives grace but not with sufficient contrition and love to satisfy for the penalty, that soul then goes through the pains of **purgatory**."

"In **purgatory**, souls pass through the second and last means of satisfaction...Through the light of conscience, they receive the gift of grace."

"So, you see the satisfaction is made through the desire of the soul united to Me, who is the infinite good, in a greater or lesser degree to create according to the measure of love obtained in the desire and prayer of the recipient."

"Increase the fire of that desire and let not a moment pass without crying to Me with a humble voice or without continual prayer for Me or your neighbors."

"Bear yourselves with meaningful courage and make yourself dead to all of your sensuality."

5. HOW PLEASING TO GOD IS THE WILLING DESIRE TO SUFFER FOR HIM

"The more the soul endures, the more it shows, the more the soul loves Me."

"With an increase in love grows sorrow and pain; therefore, the soul that grows in love, grows in sorrow."

"If the soul elects to love Me, the soul should elect to tolerate pain for Me in whatever form or circumstance I may send to that soul."

"Therefore, bear yourselves with meaningful courage for unless you do so, you will not prove yourself to be spouses of My truth."

"Ask and it will be given to you for I deny nothing to a person who asked Me in truth."

"The love of divine charity is so closely joined to the soul with perfect patience that neither can leave the soul without the other."

"Patience cannot be proved in any other way than by suffering. Patience is united with Me."

6. VIRTUE OBTAINED BY NEIGHBOR'S DEFECTS

"Every act of assistance that one performs should proceed from the love which one has through love of Me."

"Every evil derives from the soul's deprivation of love for Me and one's neighbor. Evil is done to oneself and your neighbor, not against Me. No evil can touch Me except as I count done to Me that which one does to oneself."

"I say, you are all obligated to help one another by word, doctrine, good works, or any other needs."

"Sin causes physical and mental injury. The sinner conceives pleasure in the idea of sin and hatred of virtue. It is pleasure from sensual selfishness which deprives the soul of love, which one ought to have toward Me and one's neighbor."

"One should remind oneself and others of love of virtue and hatred of vice, which if one doesn't, it is cruelty toward one's neighbors and makes oneself an instrument to destroy life and give one to death."

"Pride through love of one's own reputation produces hatred of one's neighbor, reputing oneself to be greater than the neighbor. That is an injury done to that neighbor...It is a positive act of sin to deprive your neighbor of that which you ought to give that person."

"Every sin done against Me is done through the medium of the neighbor."

7. VIRTUES BY MEANS OF NEIGHBORS NEEDS

"Perverse selfishness has poisoned the entire world and has weakened the Mystical Body of the Holy Church."

"Love gives life to all virtues because no virtue can be obtained without love, which is pure love for Me."

"When the soul knows its own humanity, it finds humility and hatred of its own sensual passions and learns a perverse law. The soul is bound up in its members and fights against itself."

"The soul attributes to Me through humility that knowledge it has obtained of itself by My grace. I have drawn the soul out of darkness and lifted it up into the light of true knowledge."

"As the soul loves Me, the soul loves its neighbor because love toward a neighbor issues from Me."

"Endurance of suffering alone without desire is not sufficient to punish a fault."

"One can only be of use in one's state in life who is bound to Me with love."

8. VIRTUES ARE PROVEN AND FORTIFIED BY THEIR OPPOSITES

"A person proves patience by the neighbor when that person receives injuries from that neighbor...bestowing humility on a proud person, faith and kindness on a cruel person, and benignity and gentleness on an irascible person."

"Virtues of a person are not diminished by evil denunciation of virtue but brings human beings to love and desire for the salvation of souls."

"Virtue is not only proved in those who render good for evil but that many times a good person gives back fiery coals of love which dispel the hatred of an angry heart. From hatred often follows benevolence by virtue of the love and perfect patience which is in the person who sustains the anger of the wicked bearing and supporting ones defects."

"If one observes the virtues of fortitude and perseverance these virtues are proved by the endurance of the injuries of a wicked person, who by injuries or flatteries constantly endeavors to turn one from following the doctrine of truth."

"Fortitude, if not being tested by many contraries, would not be a serious virtue found in truth."

II. DISCRETION

#10. PARABLE OF LOVE

"The affection of love is in the soul"

"The soul can only live by love"

UTILITY TO ONE'S NEIGHBOR

GRACE + VIRTUE

DISCRETION

FIRST LOVE GOD

FRUIT + FLOWERS

BRANCHES

Humility
=
Obedience
↑
Patience
↑
GOD'S LOVE

SOUL
(Infinite)
-Memory
-Intellect
-Free Will

TRUNK
(Finite)

SOIL
Soul's Humility

CREATOR
ALL GOOD
PERFECT CHARITY

ROOT
God the Father

GOD IS THE CIRCLE OF TRUE KNOWLEDGE NEVER ENDING

TREE OF LOVE AND LIFE

"Knowledge of oneseslf and of Me is found in the earth of humility."

"Patience proves that I am in the soul"

"Object of a soul's creation is glory and praise to My Name."

II. TREATISE OF DISCRETION

Sections 9-48

9. AN AFFECTION OF LOVE SHOULD NOT RELY ON PENANCE

"Affection of love should not place its reliance chiefly on penance but rather on virtue and receive its life from humility and render to each man his due."

"Penance performed alone without virtue would please Me little."

"Discretion receives life from humility and renders to each man his due."

"The soul should place reliance on the affection of love with holy hatred of itself accompanied by true humility and perfect patience together with hunger and desire for My honor and My salvation of souls."

"The soul should place its principal affections in virtue rather than penance."

"Virtue is rooted in the truth, but the soul needs to acquire knowledge of oneself and of Me."

"Humility proceeds from self-knowledge."

"Know that the soul does not exist of itself but is in existence because of grace from Me."

"The virtue of discretion develops on self-knowledge and indiscretion. Pride robs Me of the honor due to Me."

"Self-knowledge produces humility for each human being and should allow one to do things for one's neighbor discreetly and lovingly."

"The virtues of self-knowledge and humility are bound and mingled together."

10. A PARABLE OF A TREE FROM ITS ROOTS TO FRUIT

Creator-roots: Soul-soil: God's Commands-Trunk: Discretion-branches: Virtues-flowers: Graces-fruits: (The images of the Tree of Love and Life were inspired by this parable.)

"This parable demonstrates how love, humility and discretion are united."

"The three virtues are depicted as if a circle were drawn on the surface of the earth with a tree in the center. Consider in the same way the soul is a tree existing by love...if the soul does not have the divine love of perfect charity the soul will die. The soul should grow from the circle of true knowledge which is contained in Me who like a circle has no beginning or end. Knowledge of oneself and of Me is found in the earth of true humility... the tree of love feeds itself on humility bringing forth from its trunk the branches of true discretion...through the affection of love in the soul."

"Patience proves that I am in the soul and the soul in Me."

"The soul renders the fruit of grace and the utility to one's neighbor according to the zeal of those who come to receive fruit from My servants. To Me the soul renders the sweet odor of glory and praise to My Name fulfilling the object of the soul's creation. Fruits cannot be taken from the soul without the soul's will in as much as they are all flavored with discretion because they are all united."

11. PENANCE IS AN INSTRUMENT TO ARRIVE AT VIRTUE

"Penance and other corporal exercises are to be taken as instruments for arriving at virtue and not as a principal affection of the soul. The light of discretion develops in various modes and operations."

CATHERINE'S QUESTION:

"What can I do to endure suffering for Thee, Oh Lord?"

GOD THE FATHER'S REPLY:

"I take delight in few words and many works."

"Corporal mortification does not give Me much pleasure. It is courageous works of endurance with patience of virtuous acts intrinsic to the soul producing fruits that are worthy of grace."

"Words equal finite works, and I seek infinite works that are perfections of love rather than corporal exercises."

"Words accompanied by true discretion can be an act of love. Corporal works would receive no merit and would only offend Me...Words are considered to be a means but not an infinite end."

"Mortify the body to destroy self-will to combat with the spirit in an effort to annihilate everything selfish and be subject to My will through the virtue of discretion."

"Merit consists in the virtue of love alone, flavored with the light of true discretion, without which the soul is worth nothing."

"Love should be directed to Me endlessly and boundlessly since I am the Supreme and Eternal Truth."

"Holy discretion ordains that the soul should direct all of its powers to My service with manly zeal. The soul should love its neighbor with such devotion that the soul would lay down a thousand times, if it were possible, the life of its body for the salvation of souls enduring pain and torment so that its neighbor may have a life of grace, giving the soul temporal sustenance for the relief of its body."

"Holy discretion is prudence, which cannot be cheated by fortitude, which cannot be a perseverance from end-to-end, stretching from heaven to earth—that is, from knowledge of Me to knowledge of oneself, from love of Me to love of others."

"Virtue and love are conceived through discretion; if not, they are without merit, even if they are performed for a neighbor."

12. THE SOUL GROWS BY MEANS OF A DIVINE RESPONSE

"The soul's dignity is its creation in the image and likeness of God and has been given that which is not its due."

"The mirror of the soul is the goodness of God, who knows its own indignity due to the consequences of its actions through sensuality."

"Death of the soul would have occurred had it not been for the strength of God, purified by divine love, as well as hunger for the salvation of the world and for the reformation of the Holy Church."

Prayer of Moses:

"Lord! Have mercy for my people that You created in Your own image so that human people might participate in everything belonging to You."

Catherine states: "Through the intellect, the soul might come to know You, seeing Your goodness. The soul might participate in the wisdom of Your only begotten Son through the clemency of the Holy Spirit."

"You the Eternal God gave humanity means of reconciliation so that after the Great Rebellion into which the souls had fallen, there should come a greater peace. You gave humanity Your only begotten Son to be the mediator between us and You."

13. GOD GRIEVES FOR CHRISTIANS

"I gave the Blood of Christ for the salvation of mankind. A soul who receives it must properly dispose oneself to receive it in proportion to his or her disposition and affection. To the one living in iniquity and the darkness of mortal sin, one gets death, not life, unless one corrects oneself with contrition and repentance."

"All of you vessels made of the corrupted clay of Adam were not disposed to eternal life because of the sins of the souls of mankind. My divine mercy through My only begotten Son corrected the sin of Adam and satisfied the whole human race by the fire of divine love... destroying the stain of Adam's sin, Jesus Christ gave life to the debilitated souls who are guilty of the original sin."

"The stain of the original sin is not entirely removed by holy baptism but has the virtue of a conversion to a life of grace by means of that glorious, precious Blood."

"The soul by freewill chooses good or evil. No demon or creature can constrain that soul to one smallest fault without consent."

14. SIN PRE-PASSION OF CHRIST WAS PUNISHED LESS THAN POST-PASSION: GOD PROMISES MERCY TO THE WORLD AND TO THE HOLY CHURCH

"Mercy is extended to the Holy Church by the prayers and sufferings of its servants. Humanity is not grateful for the Blood of My Son, when I desired nothing other than sanctifying grace since the stain of Adam's sin is taken away."

"Humanity was closely bound to Me through its being, which I have given to it in My own image and likeness. Humanity was bound to render glory to Me, but humanity deprived Me of it, and humanity gave it to itself...Thus humanity transgressed My obedience that was imposed on it. It became My enemy."

"I took your humanity. I freed you from the service of the devil. I made you free."

"Humanity has become God, and God has become human through the union of the divine with human nature. It has been procreated to grace...It is now obligated to render Me glory and praise by following in the steps of My Incarnate Word."

"Mankind must repay Me the debt of love to Myself and to its neighbor with true and genuine virtue."

"If it does not do it, the greater will be its debt due to the offense, and therefore by divine justice, the greater its suffering in eternal damnation. The Christians will be greater than the pagans."

"A soul's beauty can be restored peacefully by humble and continued prayer, by the sweat and tears shed by the fiery desire of My servants. You will not fear the world's persecution for I will protect you through My divine providence. I shall never fail you in the slightest need."

15. GOD MADE HIS SON A BRIDGE BY WHICH HUMANITY CAN CROSS

"The road was broken that no one could arrive at eternal life. People did not render Me glory as I created them."

"The souls of people found themselves rebelling against themselves. They transgressed My obedience and produced weariness and trouble for themselves with the devil in the world. Wishing to remedy the disobedient souls' great evils, I have given to them the bridge of My Son."

16. GOD INDUCES THE SOUL TO LOOK AT THE GREATNESS OF THIS BRIDGE

"The intellect will see the difference of the perfect that follow in truth, who have sorrow for the damnation of the ignorant with the difference being those who walk in the light and those who walk in the dark."

"The bridge reaches from heaven to earth and constitutes the union which I have made with humanity."

"The sacrifice of My only begotten Son offered to Me to take death from you and give life to you...In order that humanity might come to its true happiness with the angels."

SAINT CATHERINE'S PRAYER TO GOD:

"I am the thief, and You have been punished for me... Show me how to cross the bridge."

17. THE THREE STEPS OF THE BRIDGE

ONE - "The soul is the wood of the cross."

TWO - "Through the cross, 'I am lifted on high I will draw all things to Me.'"

THREE - "Greater love I could not show you than to lay down My life for you."

18. BRIDGE COMPONENTS

"The bridge built of stones signifies virtue. There is food found on the bridge for those who go over the bridge, who obtain life in heaven; who goes under, death and hell."

"Heaven was locked before the crucifixion...Justice did not let souls pass over."

"Virtues are the stone built by Christ, who gives virtues by His grace through His doctrine. Jesus's Blood is the 'mortar' that holds the 'stones' of virtue together."

"Heaven was opened by the key of His Blood."

"Through His mercy and through His ministers of the Holy Church, who give bread and wine to sustain His creatures on their journey across the bridge as pilgrims to get to the door."

"I am the way, the truth, and the life. He who follows Me does not walk in darkness, but light."

"You who follow the truth receive a life of grace and with that truth, destroy the lie that the devil told Eve."

"The devil broke up the road to heaven, and the truth brought the pieces together again and cemented them with His Blood. Those following this road will pass through the door of truth and find themselves united to Me, who is the door and the road at the same time to infinite peace."

"He who goes under the bridge and into the water with no stones to support himself drowns."

"The problem of disordinate love of creatures is that by loving them, it prevents them from loving Me; therefore, the soul drowns and is sentenced to death."

"Sons of the devil, who is the father of lies, have passed through the door of falsehood. They receive eternal damnation."

19. TRAVELERS ON BOTH SIDES OF THE BRIDGE AND RIVER CAN HAVE PROBLEMS

"He is a fool indeed who despises so great a good and chooses rather to receive in this life the earnest money of hell, walking by the lower road with great toil and without any advantage...Through their sins, they are deprived of Me, who is the Supreme and Eternal Good."

20. ON THE ASCENSION, THE BRIDGE DID NOT LEAVE THIS EARTH

"To the apostles looking up to heaven, the angel said; 'Do not stand here any longer for He is seated at the right hand of the Father.'"

"The power of the Holy Spirit is one thing with Me the Father and with My Son."

"Thus, through the bodily presence of My Son leaving you, His doctrine and the stones of virtue founded upon His doctrine, which is the way made for you by this bridge."

"The clemency of the Holy Spirit made you certain of the doctrine of the crucified Christ, providing mankind a path for forgiveness of sins."

"I made the body of Christ a bridge by the union of the divine with human nature; this is the truth."

"The doctrine is found in the Mystical Body of the Holy Church as a lifeboat to save an errant soul."

"He is the way, the truth, and the life."

"I will return you. I will not leave you as orphans but will send you the Paraclete coming as the Holy Spirit."

"I will send to you the lanterns of the Holy Church, apostles, martyrs, confessors, evangelists, and holy doctors of the church, from whom humanity can learn the doctrine."

"For in His bodily presence, He will not return until the last day of judgement. He will judge the world to render good to the virtuous and reward them for their labors in both body and soul and to dispense eternal death to those who have lived wickedly in the world."

"For sinners, I beg you to pray to Me for who I am, asking you to give your tears and sweat that you may receive My mercy."

21. CATHERINE'S PRAYER - GIFTS AND GRACES BY GOD TO HUMANITY

"God said, 'Those who abandon mortal sin and return to Me, because of My mercy, I don't remember that you have offended Me. Then Catherine continued, 'Humanity's sin destroyed the bodily life of the Immaculate Lamb... who conquered death by God's mercy and shines in Your saints...Your mercy even constrains You to give more to humanity in the sacrifice of the Mass and the Eucharist so we, the weak ones, would have comfort and the ignorant commemorating You would not lose the memory of Your benefits.'"

22. VICE PRODUCES A SOUL'S DEATH

"If you produce mortal sin in your mind and carry it out, you lose the gift of grace because the disordinate love of the world is dead to grace...If the eye of the intellect does not know My truth, the intellect has no object before it except itself with the dead love of its own sensuality."

"This corpse is dead to grace. Only free will remains as long as the body lives. Humans can never help themselves while in mortal sin. Slaves of sin signify the height of pride and nourish it by their own selfishness, impatience, indiscretion, and pride. The worm of conscience, full of ingratitude for My love and mercy, can only be changed into a state of sanctifying grace by asking for My forgiveness. One must be grateful for the benefits given to that soul using the intellect and free will to be saved from drowning in the river during human life."

23. FRUITS OF THE TREE ARE AS DIVERSE AS SINS:

FIRST THE SIN OF SEXUALITY

"Oh, ugly souls, who were made sisters to the angels, and now you have become brute beasts. The sin of sexuality

takes away the light of the intellect like no other sin...
The ignorant and false Christians, who do not recognize
sexuality, lose grace by the sin of such filthy action."

24. EVIL THAT FOLLOWS FROM AVARICE

"Avarice proceeds from pride and always carries with
it the thought of its own reputation, opinion, vainglory,
vanity of heart, and boasting in that which does not
belong to it. Avarice rings for that deceitful heart that
is neither pure nor liberal, making a person show one
thing with his or her tongue while another in his or her
heart. It makes one conceal the truth and tell lies for
one's own profit, which also produces envy and does
not let the miser have any happiness out of his or her
own or others' good."

"I call the soul heaven because I made the soul alive at
first by grace hiding Myself while making a mansion for
the soul through the affection of love."

"When the soul has separated itself from Me, like an
adulteress loving herself and creatures more than Me,
the soul makes a god of itself, persecuting Me with
many diverse sins."

"Self-love means selfishness, seen as pride, which
through avarice, feeds on its own sin."

25. AUTHORITY CAN PRODUCE INJUSTICES

"People who hold their heads high according to
their authority use injustice against Me, against their
neighbor, and against themselves by not paying their
debt of virtue.."

"Ultimately, they are bound to pay their debt to Me through honor, glory, and praise...Jewish high priests condemned Jesus and ignored My Son when He said, 'The kingdom of God is among you'...They lost their light of reason."

"Sometimes avarice can become so prudish that people might not consider their children and relatives falling into great misery. Nevertheless, through My great mercy, I sustain them so that they can repent of their sins."

26. FALSE JUDGEMENTS PRODUCE INDIGNITIES

"Against Jesus, the charges by the fourteen high priests were indicative that these men were working by virtue of Beelzebub...Envy, perverse rashness, and impatience all produce a rotten heart and slavery to sin."

"Sin is nothing to the devil. Beelzebub is a product of sin."

"Christ's death on the cross, imposed on Jesus by God the Father, through obedience erased the disobedience of Adam. God's only begotten Son's pain through the crucifixion beat out all vice through an ultimate act of love."

"Through injustice and false judgement, the world was reproved when I sent the Holy Spirit on the apostles, and again it will be reproved on the last day of judgement. This was meant by My Truth when He said, 'I will send the Paraclete, who will reprove the world for injustice and false judgement.'"

"The Holy Spirit is one with Me, and I with My only begotten Son."

27. THREE CORRECTIONS FOR THE WORLD

"The **first** was given when the Holy Spirit came down on the disciples, and they were fortified by My power at Pentecost."

"The **second** occurred when the doctrine of My truth was corrected by My Son through the spoken word of the apostles."

"The **third** is the continuous corrections that I make to the world by means of the Holy Scriptures."

"This continuous preaching of My servants, putting the Holy Spirit on their tongue to announce My truth, even as the devil puts himself on the tongues of the servants."

"They cannot say, 'I had no one reprove Me,' because the truth is revealed to them showing them vice and virtue."

SAINTS: "Paul, My glorious star and standard bearer, and all the saints, who have been tormented with pain I permitted for the increase of grace and virtue in their souls to obtain eternal life."

SINNERS: "At corporal death, arise ye dead and come to judgement! Those who followed the temptations of the devil, bring yourself to eternal damnation."

28. INJUSTICE AND FALSE JUDGEMENT

"A condemnation of the soul that has arrived at an end where there can be remedy at the extreme of death, where the worm of conscience, which I told you was blinded by self-love...This soul can still find mercy if it has the light to understand through an act of sincere contrition because of the offense perpetrated against Me. That soul can still be forgiven."

"If the act of contrition occurs because of the fear of pain in hell and not that I was offended personally, that soul will be condemned to eternal damnation...Where Judas's suicidal hanging displeased Me more than Peter's betrayal by denial of knowing My Son, Jesus, but who 'wept bitterly' with deep regret, leading Me to forgive Peter."

"Those souls that depreciate My mercy, I justify sending them to hell with the devil, as his servant, because of their own sensuality and selfishness. They are eternally damned because they have offended Me."

29. TORMENTS OF THE DEVIL

"Their contrition was not sincere for the offense done to Me. By not relying on My divine mercy and sorrow only for their own pain, they receive eternal punishment."

"The most significant torments are the deprivation of visualizing Me and a worm of conscience that produces an inability to communicate with Me."

"Presence of the devil allows one to know oneself better, and by one's sin, one has made oneself worthy of the devil."

"Hell's fire produces continuous burning that doesn't consume souls."

30. FINAL JUDGEMENT DAY - THIRD REPROOF

"Confusion and shame will generate because of an intolerable reproof in the miserable soul that is increased by the union that the soul will make with the body."

"The Son will come to reprove the world with divine power, who on earth, God the Father, left Him to suffer like a man to satisfy your guilt."

"The Son will come in His own person and will render to everyone his or her due. There will be no one on that day who will not tremble."

"To the damned, He will produce torment and terror; to the just, it will cause the fear of reverence with great joy. He will come to judge the world through its own defects."

31. DIFFERENCES BETWEEN JUST AND DAMNED SOULS

"The damned cannot desire any good because their hatred is so great. They continue to blaspheme Me because the life of that human was ended, and free will was bound."

"If human beings finish their lives dying in hatred with the guilt of mortal sin, especially if they have been the cause of damnation to others, they most certainly will be among the damned."

"For the just soul whom life finishes in the affection of charity and bonds of love, the soul is measured according to the measure with which it has come to Me."

"They rejoice and exult, participating in each other's goodness with the angels with whom they are placed according to their diverse and various virtues in the world, all being bound in the bonds of love."

"The soul's free will is bound in the bond of love in such a way that time failing it and dying in a state of grace, it cannot sin anymore."

"Their will is so united with Mine that seeing a family member in hell does not bother them. They are even content to see them punished as My enemies. There is nothing with which they disagree with Me."

"The soul in heaven has certainty of happiness and consequently no pain of desire because no perfection is lacking in the soul after the resurrection."

"The soul gives bliss to the body; thus the soul will give up its abundance and will clothe itself on the last day of judgement in the garments of its own flesh, for which it has quilted a glorified body that can pass through a wall. Neither water or fire can injure it—not by virtue of itself but by virtue of the soul, which virtue is from Me, given the soul by grace and by the ineffable love with which I created the soul in My image and likeness."

"The happiness which the glorified body takes in the glorified humanity of My only begotten Son gives you an assurance of your resurrection."

"You do not wait with fear but with joy of the divine judgement. Those who finish their lives loving Me and have good will toward their neighbor will be safe because of My love and mercy."

32. AFTER GENERAL JUDGEMENT, THE PAIN OF THE DAMNED WILL INCREASE

"The Voice will say, 'Arise, you dead, and come to judgement.'"

"The soul will return with the body. The just to be glorified, and damned to be tortured eternally."

"In the Holy Gospel, it says, 'That which they should have done for their neighbor.'"

"At the time of death, only the soul is reproved. At the general judgement, the soul is reproved together with the body because the body has been the companion and an instrument of the soul to do good or evil, accordingly as the free will pleases. Every word, good or bad, is done by the means of the body."

"To the perverse ones will be rendered eternal pains by means of their bodies because their bodies were the instrument of evil."

"Their miserable sensuality with its filthiness in the vision of their nature united with the purity of My deity...By their own fault, they sunk into the deepest depth of hell."

"Go, cursed ones, to the eternal fire. Their soul and the body will be with the devil without any remedy or hope, according to their evil works on this earth."

"So the body and soul together will be punished in diverse ways. The devil is their door...Jesus said, 'No one can go to the Father except through Me.'"

"To the perverse ones will be rendered eternal pains by means of their own bodies since their bodies were the instruments of evil"

"The devil says, 'Whoever thirsts for the water of death, let him come and I will give it to him.'"

33. TEMPTATION'S SIGNIFICANCE

"Every soul sees its final place either of pain or of glory before the soul is separated from the body. The devil is the instrument of My justice to torment the souls who have miserably offended Me. I have set him in this life to tempt and molest my creatures, not for My creatures to be conquered but that they may conquer, proving their virtue received from Me, the glory of victory."

"No one should fear any battle or temptation of the devil that may come to oneself because I have made My creatures strong. I have given them strength of will, fortified in the Blood of My Son, which neither devil nor creature can move because it is yours given by Me."

"If a person does not give in to the devil's temptation and molestation, that person will never be injured by the guilt of sin but will be fortified. The eye of the intellect is opened to see My love, which allows a person to be tempted so as to arrive at virtue by being proved."

"One does not arrive at virtue except through knowledge of self and knowledge of Me."

"My goodness does not yield to these thoughts. My love permits these temptations for the devil is weak. He can do nothing unless I allow it so that you may come to a perfect knowledge of yourself and of Me. You learn through a contrary experience."

"The devil is My minister to torture the damned in hell and in life on earth improving virtue in the soul by depriving it of that which the soul cannot do unless wishing to do it...At the moment of death, they voluntarily put themselves in the devil's hand under a perverse 'lordship.' They await no other judgement than that of their own conscience coming to eternal damnation."

"The righteous who have lived in charity, virtue, faith, and perfect hope in the blood of the Lamb will taste eternal life before they have left the mortal body."

"The imperfect arrive at the place called **purgatory** with mercy and some faith."

34. THE DEVIL DECEIVES SOULS UNDER GOOD PRETENSES

"The devil invites men with the pleasure and conditions of the world."

"He catches them with the hook of pleasure under the pretense of good. If the soul didn't see good or pleasure, the soul would not allow itself to be caught. The soul of its very nature always relishes good."

"The soul, blinded by self-love, doesn't know or discern that which is truly good and of profit to the soul or body."

"The devil sees them blinded by selfishness and gives to each person in their own way that which they desire according to their condition as noble person, prelate, or religious."

"Those who care for nothing but themselves, loving themselves to the detriment of My injury, I will relate to you their end."

"They fear the thorn because they are blinded and do not know or seek the truth. They pass the thorn which appears to them to stand in the way of following the truth."

"Conscience always fights on one side and sensuality on the other."

"As soon as a person with hatred and displeasure of oneself courageously makes up one's mind, saying, 'I wish to follow Christ crucified,' then I find inestimable sweetness according to one's disposition and desire, saying, 'I am your God, unmoving and unchangeable. I do not draw away from any creature who wants to come to Me.'"

"If blinded by disordinate love, they know neither Me or themselves. They cannot escape enduring pain. No one can pass through this life without a cross. This world germinates trials and tribulations that are overcome not by self-love but of holy desire."

35. EVERYONE PASSES THROUGH THIS LIFE WITH PHYSICAL OR MENTAL PAIN

"My servant bears pain because of free will. Saints, like Paul, do not feel the weariness of pain for their will is in accord with Mine. It is the will that gives trouble to mankind. Those who are the devil's servants taste the earnest money of hell. My servants taste the earnest money of heaven."

"My servants are blessed by seeing and knowing Me, in which their vision and knowledge are fulfilled even on this earth because the will is satisfied. Knowing Me, they have seen My goodness in themselves, and through their intellect, the eye of the soul illuminates the knowledge of My truth."

"The eye of the pupil of most holy faith, which light of faith enables the soul to know and to follow the doctrine of My truth, the Word Incarnate."

Without the pupil of faith, one could not visualize My truth. People whose intellect is infused with self-love are blinded to My truth."

"My servants suffer corporally but not mentally. A sensitive will is dead, which gives pain and afflicts the mind of the creature."

"They bear everything with severance, deeming themselves favored in having tribulations for My sake, and they desire nothing but what I desire."

"If people experience infirmity, tribulation, poverty, and loss of loved ones, and they endured them within the light of reason and holy faith, realizing that I permit them through love and not through hatred but in reparations for their sins, understanding that by the light of faith, good must be rewarded and evil punished."

"They drive away sin with contrition of heart, and with perfect patience, their labors are rewarded with infinite good—patience because their hearts are drawn out of them and united to Me by the affection of love."

36. SAINT CATHERINE'S PRAYER FOR THE SOULS DROWNING IN THE WATER

"Oh, inestimable Love, great is the delusion of Your creatures. Please clarify and explain to me the three steps visualizing Christ on the cross to keep Your truth. Who are those who ascend the 'staircase' to cross the bridge to avoid drowning and damnation?"

37. THE BRIDGE'S THREE STEPS IDENTIFY WITH THE THREE POWERS OF THE SOUL

"I created the soul in My image and likeness with **memory, intellect, and will**."

"Every evil is founded in selfishness, which is a cloud that takes away the light of reason, which is the reason for intensifying the light of faith; when one is lost, so is the other."

"Because the soul is made for love as I have created it, so affection moves the intellect, saying 'I will love because the food on which I feed is love.'"

"The intellect, feeling itself, is awakened by affection."

"If you will love, I will give you that which you can love."

"Contemplating the misery of the soul through sin, the soul discovers My mercy, that will give it time to draw the soul out of darkness...Affection nourishes itself in love and through holy desire. The soul destroys its own sensuality, united with true humility and perfect patience."

"So, on the contrary, a sensual disease wants to love sensual things. The eye of the intellect sets before itself its sole object as a transition of things with selfish displeasure of virtue and love of vice. The soul draws pride and presents vice to the soul."

"Vice is a glittering object as the intellect sees it. Had worldly things no such brightness, there would be no sin. A person, by his or her very nature, cannot desire anything but good. Vice, appearing to the soul under the color of the soul's good, causes the soul to sin."

"The intellect's vision is deluded by vice. The intellect and will are deluded into loving them and the memory into retaining them."

"Free choice agrees with the will, and it becomes one thing with it. The soul with the will producing free choice in My name, both spiritual and temporal acts of a human, gets rid of sensuality and binds itself to reason. Then by grace, I rest in the middle of them and what Jesus said, 'When there are two or three or more gathered together in My name, there I am in the middle of them.'"

38. THREE POWERS MUST BE UNITED TO OBTAIN ETERNAL LIFE

"If you desire to arrive at eternal life, you must persevere in virtue."

"If you desire to arrive at eternal death, you must persevere in vice."

39. AN EXPOSITION ON CHRIST'S WORDS

"Whoever thirsts, let him come to Me and drink for I am the fountain of the water of life."

"He did not say 'Go;' He said, 'Come,' because in Me, the Father, there is no pain, but in My Son, there can be pain."

"Whoever follows His doctrine, perfectly or imperfectly, produces a union of the divine nature with human nature, and you also are finding yourself in Him and also in Me."

"In this mortal life, one cannot be without pain because humanity's on earth because of sin."

40. RATIONAL CREATURES EXIT A SINFUL STATE BY THE THREE STEPS OF THE BRIDGE

"Ascending the three steps of the 'bridge' is a method by which a soul can exit a sinful state and enter a virtuous existence...To be invited you must first have thirst."

"A person who doesn't thirst will not persevere. That person will turn back at the smallest prick of persecution for such a person doesn't love Me. One is afraid because one is alone. If that person had ascended the stairs, that person would not have been alone, and therefore, such a person would have been secured."

"Why two or three or more? The number one is excluded as useless. If one has no companion, I cannot be in the midst for the one who is wrapped up in selfishness is solitary."

"Why solitary one is separated from My grace, the love of one's neighbor, and by sin, that person deprives Me. Alone, we are selfish, and that is not acceptable to Me."

"The greatest commandments of the law are completely contained in two, and if these are not observed, the law is not observed."

"**The two greatest commandments:**"

"**To love Me above everything;**"

"**To love your neighbor as yourself.**"

"These are the beginning, middle, and end of the law as developed by the congregation as **the powers of the soul are memory, intellect, and will**."

"Servile fear is a state of imperfection and the first step of the 'bridge.'"

"The first step of the bridge includes:

Memory - to retain My benefits in My goodness.

Intellect - to understand My charity.

Will - to love and desire Me."

"When these three virtues and powers of the soul are working together in My Name, I am in the midst thereby grace. A person who's full of My love and that of one's neighbor's virtues produces the appetite of the soul disposed to thirst."

FIRST STEP - THIRST

"Affection stripped of self-love is mounted above the transitory things of this world along with tribulation."

SECOND STEP - LIGHT OF INTELLECT

"The soul finds peace and quiet because the memory is filled with My love."

"The soul finds itself accompanied by Me and walks safely."

THIRD STEP - FOUNDATION OF THE WATER OF LIFE

"The soul has an empty vessel in the hand of all the pleasures and affections of this world. It fills itself with love of celestial things and sweet, divine love. It then passes through the door of Christ crucified and tastes the water of life, finding the soul in Me."

41. IN A DIVINE MIRROR CREATURES WERE SEEN IN DIVERSE WAYS

"Souls feeling themselves pricked by servile fear in feeling their own personal pain and going from the first state, arriving to the second state. Few saw arrivals at the greatest of perfection."

42. SERVILE FEAR IS INSUFFICIENT FOR ETERNAL LIFE WITHOUT LOVE OF VIRTUE

"The law of fear and that of love are united."

"They have arisen with servile fear from the vomit of mortal sin, but if they do not arise with love of virtue, servile fear alone is not sufficient to give eternal life."

"Love of holy fear is sufficient because the law is founded in love and holy fear."

"The old law was the law of fear. The new law is the law of love, given by the Word of My only begotten Son, and is founded in love alone."

"The new law fulfills the old law and unites it by removing the imperfection. The fear of penalty produces a perfection of holiness, not because of the fear of damnation but of offending Me, who is the Supreme Good."

"So that the imperfect law of fear was made perfect by the law of love."

"The penalty of sins committed by humanity was taken away and not punished as it was in the old law given to Moses."

"This does not mean sin is not punished but those people punished themselves in their lives with perfect contrition. In the other life, when the soul is separated from the body, the person physically dies come the time of justice."

"In **purgatory**, the souls should arise from servile fear and arrive at love and holy fear of Me; otherwise, there is no remedy against falling back again into the "river," reaching the waters of tribulation and seeking the thorns of consolation. All consolations are thorns that pierce the soul who loves them inordinately."

43. THE SECOND STEP OF THE "BRIDGE" PERFECT STATE

Memory- the soul sees the punishment of sin.

Intellect- moves the soul to hate vice

Will- abolishing self-love with prudence and perseverance for love of Me."

"Many lose their way and commitment. They fail and do not arrive at the second step. His heart is the second step of perfection."

44. LOVING GOD FOR THEIR OWN PROFIT
IMPERFECT STATE

"Delight and consolation which they find in Me is imperfect."

"Proof of the imperfection of this love includes:
The consolation which they found in Me and a short duration of the love for their neighbor. Seeing this, I withdraw from their minds."

"My consolation allows them to fall into battles and perplexities. This allows them to come to know of themselves, realizing that they are nothing, not having graces."

"In time of battle, they fly to Me as their benefactor with true humility to give them consolation…This labor does not profit Me."

"Such a soul is imperfect because it hasn't unwound the bandages of spiritual self-love. The truth is that everything proceeds from Me."

"I give and promise to My creatures their sanctification, which is the end that I created them by the Blood of My only begotten Son. They are washed of their inequities, and they are enabled to know My truth."

"I created them in My image and likeness and recreated them to grace with the Blood of My Son, making them adopted sons of God."

"Imperfect love was given to their neighbor, the same imperfect love to Me...love that is based only on a desire for their own advantage."

"It is not enough to flee sin from fear of punishment or embrace virtue from the motive of one's own advantage. Sin should be abandoned because it is displeasing to Me, and virtue should be loved for My sake."

"I am the rewarder of every labor given to all people, according to their state of labor, prayer, and good works with perseverance to increase their virtues. They will arrive at the state of final love."

"As a servant loves his master, I will reveal Myself to them. Secrets are revealed to a friend who has become one thing with this friend and not as a servant."

"He who loves Me shall be one thing with Me and I with him. I will manifest Myself to him, and we will dwell together."

"Two bodies yet in one soul through the affection of love. Love transforms the lover into the object loved, and where two friends have one soul, there can be no secret between them. My Truth said: 'I will come and we will dwell together; this is the truth.'"

45. GOD MANIFESTS HIMSELF TO THE SOUL WHO LOVES HIM

"A soul who loves Me in truth and follows the doctrine of My sweet amorous words participates in My manifestations to those souls in proportion to a soul's unique ability."

"Those who live in the ordinary grace of God recognize My diverse benefits."

"Souls in filial love with Me develop a sentiment of the soul by which they taste, know, and feel it. I am no acceptor of creatures. I am an acceptor of holy desires."

"Love of your neighbor produces desire and royal virtues that allow a soul through the intellect to understand the fire of divine charity."

46. CHRIST DID NOT SAY, "I WILL MANIFEST MY FATHER," BUT HE SAID, "I WILL MANIFEST MYSELF.

"He said, 'He who loves Me shall be one thing with Me' and I will manifest Myself.'"

"By following His doctrine with the affections of love, you are united with Him, and being united with Him, you are united with Me because We are one thing together."

"Reasons for not saying 'My father.'"

"He and I are one" (not separated). He said to Phillip, 'Who sees Me, sees the Father and who sees the Father sees Me. The Father has manifested Himself to Me because I am one thing with Him. I will manifest to you by means of Myself, He, and I."

"I, being invisible, could not be seen by you until you should be separated from your body. From now until the resurrection, you can see with the eye of the intellect alone for as I am, you cannot see Me now."

47. SOULS ACCESS THE BRIDGE - STEP ONE TO STEP TWO

"In the beginning humanity served Me imperfectly through servile fear but by exercise and perseverance. A person arrives at the love of delight, finding his or her own delight and profit in Me, which I call filial love."

"Filial love is perfect; a friend grows into a son."

"Every perfection and every virtue proceed from charity. Charity is nourished by humility and, hatred of self-love and sensuality through knowledge of oneself."

"A soul must persevere through self-knowledge, in which a person will learn of My mercy, through the Blood of My only begotten Son by extirpating self-will, both spiritual and temporal, in a torment of tears, as did Peter after the sin of denying knowing My Son. Yet his laminations were imperfect until after the Ascension. Then Peter and the others remained in fear until they arrived at true love, when the Holy Spirit came to them at Pentecost, as I had promised them."

"They persevered in fasting and in humble, continual prayer, receiving the Holy Spirit. At last, their fear vanished, and they preached Christ crucified."

"The forty days between ascension and Pentecost, between imperfect love, the withdrawal of Myself from time to time, not in grace but in feeling; My Truth showed you this when He said to the disciples, 'I will go and I will return to you.'"

"In order to raise the soul from imperfection, I will withdraw Myself from the soul's sentiment, depriving the soul of former consolation."

"The soul perseveres with humility in the home of knowledge with lively faith until the coming of the Holy Spirit."

"Mortal sin separates the soul from Me. The soul, when self-knowledge occurs and holy confession is obtained, then I return to the soul by grace. Then I withdraw Myself from the soul by sentiment, which I do to humiliate the soul and cause it to see Me in truth, proving to the soul to seek Me in truth and in the light of faith, developing prudence."

"If the soul loves Me without thought of self with lively faith and hatred of sensuality, the soul deems itself worthy of peace and quietness of mind."

"Though the soul perceives that I have withdrawn Myself, the soul does not look back but perseveres with humility and remains to continue with self-knowledge and lively faith."

"I leave the soul so that it may see the soul deprived of consolation and afflicted by pain. The soul may recognize its own weakness through knowledge of its imperfect love so that perfect love may be obtained by reproof of self-love."

"Awaiting Me is not done in idleness but in continual prayer, both physically and intellectually, with an alert mind in the light of faith, removing wandering thoughts of the heart through My charity. I desire nothing more than the soul's sanctification, which is certified in the Blood of My Son. The eye thus watches, illuminated by the knowledge of Me and of the soul, through continual prayer of holy desire with actual prayer according to the orders of the Holy Church."

48. IMPERFECT LOVE OF NEIGHBOR INDICATES IMPERFECT LOVE OF GOD

"Souls who have received My love sincerely without any self-regarding considerations, I satisfy the thirst of their love for their neighbor equally and sincerely."

"I require that you should love Me with the same love with which I love you. This indeed you cannot do because I loved you without being loved."

"All the love you have for Me you owe Me so that it is not because of grace that you love Me but because you ought to do so. I owe you grace; I do not owe you My love...To Me in person, you cannot repay the love which I require of you; therefore, I have placed you in the midst of your fellow human beings that you may do to them which you cannot do to Me; that is to say, you may love your neighbor free of grace without expecting any return from your neighbor. That you do to your neighbor, I count as done to Me."

This love must be sincere because it is with the same love with which you love Me that you must love your neighbor."

"IMPERFECT LOVE:
"The lover feels pain. It appears to one that the object of one's love does not satisfy
A person sees the beloved one's conversation turned away from them
The lover is deprived of consolation
Another is loved more than the lover
The root of selfishness has not been removed
The love is so weak because of self-love."

"I often permit such a love to exist so that a soul may understand the imperfection of love through self-evaluation and knowledge, following which I return to the soul with light and knowledge of My truth in proportion to the degree in which the soul defers to grace the power of slaying the soul's own will."

"Rooting out the thorns of evil thought replacing them with stones of virtue cemented in the Blood of Christ crucified, allegorically on the journey across the bridge of Christ My only begotten Son."

III. PRAYER→PERFECT LOVE

Perfect love is found in the Creator of the universe
who provided humanity with an infinite soul, composed
of memory, intellect, and free-will with the ability to acquire
and coordinate gifts of obedience, patience and humility to first
develop a love of God, the Creator, by praising honoring and
giving glory to Him and second through the ulility of one's
neighbor who is to be loved as one loves oneself.

TREE OF LOVE AND LIFE

III. TREATISE OF PRAYER

Sections 49-80

49. PURE AND GENEROUS LOVE ATTAINED BY SOULS

"The doctrine of Christ crucified produces methods of obtaining pure love through true love and the hatred of vice."

"Both through self-knowledge producing the ability to develop pure love through separation and constant prayer entirely free from consolations of the world."

"Both out of fear from knowledge of one's own imperfections and the desire to arrive at pure and generous love."

"Through a lively faith for My arrival through grace recognized by:
Never turning back for anything, except out of obedience or charity
To avoid the devil entering the soul, use vocal prayer
The soul defends itself from every adversary it grasps with the hand of love by the arm of holy faith The arm of free choice with the light of holy faith."

50. VOCAL AND MENTAL PRAYER AT THE EUCHARIST

"Prayers can be thwarted by:
Human fragility - Through the thoughts or movements of the body.
Satanic illusion - Through the words or actions of other creatures."

"By humble, continual, and faithful prayer, the soul acquires with time and perseverance every virtue."

"Holy prayer through knowledge of oneself and Me by the eye of the intellect in the light of faith and the abundance of My charity is visible to you through My only begotten Son. The Eucharist is food that strengthens little or more according to the desire of the recipient, whether one receives it sacramentally or virtually."

"Sacramentally - Host at communion provided by a minister."

"Virtually - Communication by desire of communion through contemplation of the Blood of Christ crucified, shed through love of Me and for the soul of the neighbor, through perseverance seasoned with most holy faith."

"Prayers that are only vocal are often only words rather than expressions of love, meaning that they provide nothing except completing psalms and paternosters, which pleases Me minimally. Do not abandon vocal prayer because it will not allow one to fall into idleness. Therefore, endeavor to elevate the mind during prayer to give love to Me; one should consider one's own defects and recognize My goodness in oneself and continue the exercise in true humility, remembering:

My charity for the remission of sins
The Blood of My only begotten Son
The broadness of My mercy."

"To avoid attempts by Satan to confuse humans, so that
the devil will say, 'Cursed that you are for I can find no
way to take you. If I put you down through confusion,
you rise to heaven on the wings of mercy, and if I raise
you on high, you humbly persecute me when I go to hell
so that I will not return to you anymore because you
strike me with the stick of charity.'"

SAINT CATHERINE'S PRAYER OF CONTRITION

"I confess to my Creator that my life has indeed passed
in darkness, but I will hide in the wounds of Christ
crucified and bathe myself in His Blood. My iniquities be
consumed, and with desire, I will rejoice in my Creator...
Never think through pride of your confession there is no
further need for continued forgiveness...John the Baptist
never sinned and was sanctified in his mother's womb. I
now have committed many sins and have hardly begun
to know them with sorrow and true contrition, seeing
who God is, who is offended by me, and who I am who
offended Him."

"Vocal prayer is of use to the soul who makes it pleasing Me;
even though imperfectly exercised with perseverance,
the soul will arrive at perfect mental prayer."

"Sometimes the gift of mental prayer is given to a soul.
The soul should abandon vocal prayer if the soul is able,
but when appropriate, resume vocal prayer. These
thoughts are not satisfactory for the divine office of the
clerics and religious."

"They who pray with little prudence and without method taste little, and those who proceed with significant method and prudence taste much."

"The more the soul tries to loosen its affection from itself and fasten it to Me with the light of the intellect, the more the soul knows, and the more the soul knows, the more the soul loves."

"Thus, perfect prayer is not attained through many words but through affection of desire, the soul raising itself to Me with knowledge of the soul and of My mercy, seasoned of the one with the other."

"Charity commands for the salvation of the neighbor, each one according to one's condition ought to exert oneself for the salvation of souls. It is the root of a holy will, which by words or deeds toward the salvation of one's neighbor is virtual prayer. As St. Paul said, 'He who ceases not to work, ceases not to pray.'"

Types of Prayer:

"Actual prayer, vocal, mental or charity is continual good will of one's neighbor, friendly to filial love."

"The soul will remain tepid and imperfect unless it keeps constantly in a 'perfect path.' It will only love Me and the soul's neighbor in proportion to the pleasure which the soul finds in My service."

51. FIRST STATE OF LOVE: IMPERFECT (Friendly)

"Requires knowledge of Me; otherwise, the soul becomes confused. The soul should develop a hate toward its own sensitive pleasure and delight in its consolations. With hatred founded in humility, the soul will become strong against attacks by the devil and against the persecutions by one's fellow human beings, particularly toward Me. For the soul's own good, I withdraw delight from the soul's mind."

"The soul who wishes to rise above imperfection should await My providence in the house of self-knowledge with the light of faith — the apostles prior to Pentecost."

"The intellect fastened on the doctrine of My truth with the soul will become humble because the soul will know itself in humble and continual prayer with holy and true desire."

52. SECOND STATE OF LOVE: PERFECT (Filial)

'The Apostles after Pentecost came forth from the house and fearlessly announced the doctrine of My Word by My only begotten Son, not fearing pain but rather glorifying the moment."

"They did not mind going before the tyrants of the world to announce to them the truth for the glory and praise of My Name."

"The soul who has awaited Me in self-knowledge receives Me on My return to the soul with the fire of charity and perseverance, conceived in virtue by the affection of love, participating in My power and the soul's virtue, overrode and conquered the soul's own passions, and with the eye of the intellect, participates in the wisdom of My Son."

THIRD STATE OF LOVE (Unconditional Love of Neighbor)

"The soul during the third state at the time of a neighbor's needs, the soul loses the fear of being deprived of its own consolations, which the soul conceives through the affection of love."

FOURTH STATE OF LOVE (Unitive Love with God)

"Charity is given to the neighbor who desires to form a perfect union with Me. These two states are united—i.e. one cannot be without the other for there cannot be love of Me without love of your neighbor nor love for the neighbor without love of Me."

53. IMPERFECT SOULS FOLLOW THE FATHER: PERFECT SOULS FOLLOW THE SON

"Perfect souls place none other before the eye of the intellect than Christ crucified."

"Imperfect souls, imperfect in My love, do not wish to suffer pain but only have the delight which they find in Me."

"The body of Christ crucified through the steps that a soul can take."

"First - Climb to the feet with the feet of the soul's affection."

"Second - To the side, where the soul finds the secret of the heart and knows the baptism of water, which has virtue through the Blood...where the soul unites itself with the Blood of the Lamb."

"My desire toward the human generation had ended and had finished the actual work of bearing pain and torment, and yet, I had not been able to show finite things because My love was infinite. How much more love had I wished you to see in the secret of your heart, showing it to you openly so that you might see how much more I loved than I could show you by finite pain."

"I poured from it Blood and Water to show you that the Baptism of Water is received in virtue of the Blood...For those who are not able to have a Holy Baptism with water but a Baptism of Desire satisfies the need with the affection of love."

"The soul falling into the guilt of mortal sin, by which the soul loses the grace which it drew from the Holy Baptism in virtue of the Blood, it was necessary to leave a continual Baptism of Blood."

"Divine charity provided in Holy Confession provides the soul receiving the baptism of Blood with a contrition of heart, confessing when able by My ministers who hold the keys of the Blood, sprinkling absolution upon the face of the soul."

"But if the soul is unable to confess, contrition of heart is sufficient for this baptism, the hand of My clemency giving you the fruit of this precious Blood."

"It is true that in the past, a person desiring to confess and not being able to would receive the fruit of baptism."

"But let no one be so foolish as to arrange one's deeds in the hope of receiving it so that one puts off confessing until the last extremity of death, when a person may not be able to do so."

"In My divine justice, I may say: 'You didn't remember Me in your lifetime when you could have; now I will not remember you in your death.'"

"The union of the finite and infinite can be called infinite, not that My pain nor the actuality of the body is infinite, nor the pain of the desire. I had to complete your redemption because it was terminated and finished on the cross. When the soul is separated from the body, the fruit which comes out of the pain and desire for your salvation is infinite; therefore, you receive it infinitely. Had it not been infinite, the whole human generation could not have been restored to grace, neither in the past, the present, nor the future."

"I showed you that My love was infinite by the baptism of Blood united with the fire of My charities to whomsoever will receive it, by baptism of water united with the Blood and the fire where the soul is steeped. In order to show this, it was necessary for the Blood to come out of My side."

54. WHETHER PEOPLE GIVE OR DON'T GIVE GOD GLORY, PRAISE AND HONOR

"People who do not give glory, I give them time. I use My charity and mercy, withdrawing neither on account of their sins."

"I give equally to the sinner and to the righteous person. Often, I give more to the sinner than to the righteous person, who is able to endure privation. I take from that person the goods of the world so that that person may more abundantly enjoy the goods of heaven."

"Even when sinners persecute My servants, they prove in them the virtues of patience and charity, allowing them to suffer humbly and offer to Me their persecutions and injuries. I turn them into My praise and glory...Whether they will or not render My Name with praise and glory, even when they intend to do Me infamy and harm."

55. EVEN THE DEVIL RENDERS GLORY AND PRAISE TO GOD

"Sinners are placed in this life to augment virtue in My servants, as are the devils in hell as My justiciars and augmentors of My glory; they are My instruments of justice toward the damned and the augmentors of My glory in My creatures, who are wayfarers and pilgrims on their journey to reach Me, their end."

"Their methods would be exercising in them with many temptations and taking one another's property to deprive them of charity, resulting in these things only fortifying them or producing virtues of patience, fortitude, and perseverance."

"So, you see, My truth is fulfilled in them since they render Me glory, not as citizens of eternal life, of which they are deprived by their sins, but as My justiciars, manifesting justice upon the damned and upon those in **purgatory.**"

56. THE SOUL AFTER DEATH OF THE BODY

"The soul after death has passed through this life. It sees fully the praise and glory of My Name in everything, and since the soul's pain of desire is ended, the desire is not."

"The soul who is denuded of the body and has reached Me sees it clearly and in seeing, knows the truth."

"Seeing Me, the Eternal Father, the soul loves, and in loving, the soul is satisfied! The soul also sees the injury done to Me, which before caused the soul sorrow, but it no longer can now give the soul pain but only compassion because the soul loves without pain, praying to Me continually with an affection of love so that I will have mercy on the world."

"You see then that the saints and every soul in eternal life have desire for the salvation of souls without pain because pain ended in their death, but not so the affection of love."

57. THE CONVERSION OF PAUL

"It being pleasing to My goodness a vessel was made out of him through the Eternal Trinity, I dispossessed him of Myself because no pain can fall on Me, and I wished him to suffer for My Name."

"I placed before him, as an object for the eyes of his intellect, Christ crucified, clothing him with the garment of His doctrine, binding and fettering him with the clemency of the Holy Spirit, and inflaming him with the fire of charity. Paul became a vessel, disposed of and reformed by My goodness, and on being struck, made no resistance and said to Me, 'My Lord, what do you wish me to do? Show me, which it is your pleasure for me to do, and I will do it!'"

"I illuminated him perfectly with the light of true contrition, by which he extrapolated his defects, and founded him in My charity."

58. THE SOUL'S UNITIVE STATE

"Mortal people's wills are not their own but become one with Mine. They cannot desire other than what I desire. Though they desire to be with Me, they are content to remain, if I desire them to remain, with their pain for the greater praise and glory of My Name and the salvation of souls."

"In as much as they appear to be suffering, they are rejoicing because the enduring of many tribulations is to them relief in the desire which they have for death, which oftentimes, the desire and the will to suffer pain mitigate the pain caused by them by the desire to quit the body."

"This is the third state, where they endure with patience, and bearing tribulation in glory of My Name, they rejoice seeing themselves clothed with the suffering and shame of Christ crucified."

"The eye of the intellect is lifted up and gazes into My deity when the affection behind the intellect is nourished and united with Me."

"This is a sight which I grant to the soul, infused with grace, who in truth loves and serves Me."

59. GO FOR COUNSEL FOR THE SALVATION OF THE SOUL TO A HUMBLE AND HOLY CONSCIENCE

"My saints by the Holy Scriptures, some of which were misunderstood, I illuminated them through the eye of the intellect to know the truth...Everyone receives accordingly as They are capable of being disposed to know Me for I don't despise disproportions...The intellect was before the Scriptures were formed; therefore, from the intellect developed science because in seeing, they discerned."

"The holy prophets and fathers understood, who prophesied of the coming and death of My Son. The Holy Spirit gave the apostles supernatural light. The evangelists, doctors, professors, virgins, and martyrs were all likewise illuminated by the aforesaid perfect light, each one as he or she needed it for their salvation or that of others or for the exposition of the Scriptures—the doctors' in expounding the doctrine of My truth, the preaching of the apostles, the gospels of the evangelists, the martyrs in their blood the Most Holy Faith, and the virgins in the affection of charity and purity."

"This light is seen in the Old Testament by the eye of the intellect, the prophecies, and the holy prophets. The New Testament is the word of My only begotten Son with the law of love, completing the old law by giving it love and replacing the fear of penalty by holy fear."

"Christ said, 'I come not to dissolve the law, but to fulfill it.'"

"Every light that comes from Holy Scripture comes from supernatural light. Ignorant and proud people of science are blind because their pride and cloud of selfishness (self-love) have covered up and put out the light. They are annoyed and murmur because they find much in it that appears to them to be gross and idiotic. They have lost the supernatural light, infused by grace, and they neither see nor know My goodness, nor the grace of My servants."

"It is better to obtain the counsel for the salvation of the soul to be a holy and upright conscience than to be a proud, lettered man...Who might present the Scriptures as only offering darkness."

"One may know the unitive state to be perfect, when the eye of the intellect is ravished by the fire of My charity, in which charity receives the supernatural light. The souls in the unitive state love Me because love follows the intellect, and the more it knows, the more it can love."

"The unitive state is most excellent when the soul, being yet in mortal body, tastes bliss with the immortals, and often a soul arrives at so great a union that the soul scarcely knows whether the soul is in or out of the body. It tastes the earnest money of eternal life, both because the soul is united with Me and because the soul's will is dead in Christ, by whose death the soul's union was made with Me, thus a perfect state."

"The soul who dies with a depraved will and yields to it earns damnation."

60. A DEVOUT SOUL IN THE STATE OF TEARS

"Attains knowledge from God by:
Desire to learn from the truth
One learns the truth with the light of faith

A request of the soul to God through the intellect or will God Himself manifests it to the soul and condescending in His benignity to desire, fulfills the soul's petition."

61. FIVE KINDS OF TEARS

"Tears of fear and damnation: wicked people
Tears of punishment of the soul: those who abandon sin out of fear
Tears of imperfect love: those souls who abandon sin whose tears are imperfect
Tears of love of one's neighbor: souls who have perfect love for Me without any regard for themselves: perfect weeping
Tears of sweetness to obtain peace."

"I wish you to know that all of these various graces may exist in one soul, who rising from fear and imperfect love, reaches perfect love in the unitive state."

62. THE SOUL'S TEARS

"No member of the body will satisfy the heart so much as the eye. Pain in the heart provides tears in the eye."

"If sensual, the tears:
Engender death
Caused by disordinate love distinct from the love of Me offends Me
The soul has not arrived of perfect hatred of its guilt
The eye weeps in order to satisfy a heart's grief
This fear will not provide eternal life
Fears of damnation."

"A soul proceeds with love to know itself, and My goodness begins to take hope in My mercy in which the soul's heart feels joy. Sorrow for the soul's grief mingles with joy of hope. Self-love(selfishness) is not sensual. Self-love is a spiritual love in which the soul desires spiritual consolations or loves some creature spiritually. The soul's heart is full of grief because external consolation produces tears of tender sorrow, pitying itself with spiritual compassion of self-love."

"A soul may conceive displeasure of itself and finally perfect self-hatred."

"The soul's true knowledge of My goodness with a fire of love begins to unite itself to Me by conforming its will to Mine with compassion for one's neighbor."

"The soul with hearty love of Me and its love of one's neighbor:
Grieving solely for My offenses and not the neighbor's
Not for My penalty or loss due to the body or soul.
Thanks only giving praise and glory to My Name

With humility and patience
Conforms to the Immaculate Lamb, the only begotten Son
Glory to be persecuted in My Name
Following the doctrine of truth."

"Enduring with sweet patience every pain and trouble, which I have permitted to be inflicted for the soul's salvation. Knowing truth, loving it through intellectual effort tastes My eternal deity; therefore, the soul unites to humanity."

"The heart is united with Me in love:
  Nourishing the soul in true patience
  The soul's eye is the conduit to its heart
  Endeavors to satisfy the range of the heart with
  ears of peace
  A soul of a blessed and sorrowful state
  Blessed through the union with Me
  Sorrowful for the offense being done to My goodness
  Sorrow with no impediment to a unitive state
  Necessity to bear with others and practice continuing
  to love one's neighbor
  Together with true knowledge of oneself
  Love of neighbor is developed out of love for Me
  The soul sees ineffable love by Me and loves every
  rational creature with the selfsame love with which
  the soul is loved by Me
  The soul knows it cannot repay Me for the love I
  extend to it
  The soul repays it through that which I have provided,
  which is a neighbor with the same pure love that I
  have for humanity."

"Pure love cannot be directly returned to Me because I
  have loved humanity without being loved by humanity
  before humanity existed. It was indeed love that moved
  Me to create one's soul in My own image and likeness.
  This love you cannot repay to Me, but you can pay it to
  My rational creatures."

"Loving your neighbor without consideration of your
  own advantage, whether spiritual or temporal, but
  loving one's solely for the praise and glory of My Name
  because one's neighbor has been loved by Me."

"Thus, you will fulfill the commandment of the law to love Me above everything and your neighbor as yourself."

"These two states united nourish your soul in virtue, making growth to perfection of virtue in the unitive state."

"Mortal appears immortal because the soul's perception of its own sensuality is mortified and the soul's will is dead through the union which the soul has attained with Me."

"These two states united nourish your soul in virtue, making growth to perfection of virtue in the unitive state."

"The union of the soul with Me may receive My secrets such as prophecy. This is an effect of My goodness and is given for peace of mind to nourish souls."

"The soul could slip back to a second state again, rather than grow in virtue. The soul is never so perfect in this life that the soul cannot attain a higher perfection of love."

"To further increase a grade of perfection in the last stage, which may please you by means of My grace."

63. GOD WISHES INFINITE SERVICE

"God wishes to be served as infinite, not finite. Tears produce tears of infinite value. Tears give life if they are disciplined in virtue. You asked, 'How can their value be infinite?' Not in this life, but I call them infinite because of the infinite desire of your soul."

"Selfishness dries up the soul, producing no tears, but the renovation of grace saves the soul."

"Through holy desire founded in love, exercised with desire, the eye weeps."

"But when the soul is separated from the body and has reached Me, the soul's end, it doesn't abandon desire so as to no longer yearn for Me or the neighbor's soul. Love has entered into the soul."

"I, who am the infinite God, wish to be served by you with infinite service as the only infinite thing you possess is the affection and desire of your soul."

"Infinite desire is united to tears. The soul arrives at tasting the fire of My divine charity, passing from this life into a state of love toward Me. The soul's neighbor with unitive love produces the soul's tears to fall. Faith does not cease to offer Me a soul's blessed desires without pain or physical weeping. They have evaporated to become tears of fire of the Holy Spirit."

64. THE FRUIT OF HUMANITY'S TEARS

"Human beings, who live miserably in the world making a god of created things and of their own sensuality, produce damage to their bodies and souls."

"There are as many reasons to complain as there exist different loves."

"Everything that grows in the route of selfishness is corrupt, and anything that grows from it is also corrupt."

"Selfishness is a tree on which nothing grows but fruits of death. The soul is a tree that without love cannot live. The soul who lives righteously places its root in the valley of true humility. The root of a tree planted in pride can only bear the fruit of death, known as sin."

"No actions done by a soul in mortal sin are of value in eternal life because mortal sins are not done in grace. However, such a soul should not abandon doing good works for every good deed is rewarded, and every evil deed is punished. My justice, My divine goodness grant an incomplete reward, imperfect as the action which obtains it."

"Rewards for good works for a soul in mortal sin:
Time to repent
Life of grace means of My servants
Paul's persecutions in the prayer of Saint Stephen."

"Whatever state a person may be in, he or she should never stop doing good."

"Sin is displeasing to Me and full of hatred and unkindness toward one's neighbor."

"So, if people are thieves, they rob Me of honor and take it themselves."

False Judgements:

"Directed against oneself:
Judging what I did in love to have been done in hatred.
That which I did in truth to have been done in falsehood, they condemned according to a weak intellect.
They blind the eye of the intellect with self-love.
They hide the pupil of the most holy fait which will not allow one to see or know the truth."

"Directed against one's neighbor:
The wretched person sets itself as the judge of the affection and heart of other rational creatures. When one does not know oneself
My servants always judge well because they are founded in Me, the Supreme Good."

"False judges always judge poorly because they are founded in evil. Such critics as these cause hatred, murder, and unhappiness of all kinds to their neighbors and remove themselves far away from the love of My servant's virtues."

"These unfortunate creatures do not remember that the tongue is made only to give honor to Me and conquer sins, used to love virtue and for salvation of the neighbor. Words alone have produced revolutions of states, destruction of cities, homicides, and other evils. Their hunger is insatiable, and the earth unable to satisfy them...They are always unquiet, longing for the thing they expect to satisfy them, always desiring some finite thing."

"Humanity is placed above all creatures and not beneath them. It cannot be satisfied except in something greater than itself. Greater than, there is nothing but Myself, the Eternal God! Therefore, I alone can satisfy humanity, and because humans are deprived of satisfaction by their guilt, they remain in continual, tormented pain. Weeping follows pain because of selfishness."

65. SAINT CATHERINE'S PRAYER THANKING GOD FOR THE FOUR STATES OF TEARS AND THREE PETITIONS WITH ANSWERS IN #66, #67, #,68

PRAYER: "Through Your fiery love, I beg Your grace and mercy that I may come to You truly in light and not flee far in darkness away from Your doctrine."

PETITIONS:

"How can I counsel one of Your servants when they come to me for advice?"

"Do I have a right to judge Your servants' intentions for whom I'm praying?"

"What is the sign You said a soul would receive when being visited by You?"

66. THE LIGHT OF REASON IS NECESSARY TO SERVE GOD

FIRST STATE

"Catherine asks God, 'How should I counsel someone who comes to me for advice regarding faith?'"

"Faith is given to you in baptism. Through water or desire, it is given by the light of reason you draw from Me, the true light, by means of the eye of the intellect. Life is given to you by the intellect and causes you to walk in the path of truth, arriving at Me, the True Light. Without it, you would plunge into darkness."

"The transitory nature of humanity in the world, coupled with its fragility, demands strength through the law of perversity, for which people rebel against Me, your Creator. **The law of perversity** fights lustily against the spirit, lest it be conquered by it. The soul must conquer it by virtue; however, virtue cannot be developed except by its contrary."

"Sensuality is contrary to the spirit, and yet by means of sensuality, the soul is able to prove the love which the soul has for Me, the soul's Creator, by developing anger and displeasure. The soul rises against itself."

"I created the soul in My image and likeness, accompanied by the vilest of all things, imposing on the soul the law of perversity, so that seeing in what the soul's true beauty consisted, the soul should not raise its head in pride against Me."

"The fragility of the body is the cause of humiliation to the soul and is in no way a matter for pride, but rather for true and perfect humility."

"**The law of perversity** does not make you sin but supplies a reason to make you know yourselves and the instability of the world."

"A person must possess the light of faith for without it, the soul is not in the state of grace. The soul does not know the evil of its sin and therefore cannot avoid or hate it."

"If the soul doesn't know good through virtue, the soul cannot love or desire Me either."

"I love virtue and hate vice. A person who loves vice and hates virtue offends Me and is deprived of My grace.

Vice is sensual selfishness. If one is ignorant of vice or evil and virtue, as well as Me, that person is ignorant of one's own dignity."

67. STRIVING FOR PERFECTION

SECOND STATE

"Penance and mortification vs. destruction of self-love through ones' own will produces a soul in God's own truth, striving for perfection in both cases."

"Castigation of the body doing great and severe penance can be profitable if illuminated by discretion and founded in Me. One must act with true knowledge of itself and of Me with great humility, wholly conformed to the judgement of My will where one could often offend against one's own perfection, esteeming oneself as the judge of those who do not walk in the same path or because they place all their labor and desire in the mortification of the body, rather than the destruction of their own will."

"The soul often falls into trouble by becoming tedious and unsupportable to itself. The soul does not perceive trouble because within the soul lurks the stench of pride."

"If the soul were truly humble and not presumptuous, it would be illuminated to see that, I the primary and sweet Truth, grant condition, time, and place consolations and tribulations as they may be needed for its salvation. To complete the perfection to which I have elected for the soul, it would see that I give everything through love and with love. Therefore, with reverence and love, the soul should receive everything in this second state."

68. UNITIVE STATE - PERFECT PURITY

THIRD STATE

"This unity state of the soul I permit to happen to those who do reverence, who have deemed themselves worthy of the troubles and stumbling blocks produced by the world, who have the privation of their own consolation, no matter what circumstances happened to them."

"In the light of My eternal will, that which is nothing else but good, who gives and permits trouble so that they should be sanctified in Me."

"The soul must open the eye of its intellect and fix on the light of faith, upon Christ crucified, and follow this doctrine…Who was fed at the table of holy desire, seeking My honor, the Eternal Father, and your salvation."

"I placed My Son on the battlefield to deliver you from the hand of the devil so that you might be free from hell and taught you His doctrine so that you might open the door to heaven."

"Do not be negligent to follow Me. Laying down yourselves to rest in selfishness and ignorance, presuming to serve Me in your own way instead of the way which I have made you for by means of the Incarnate Word…No one can reach Me, the Father, if not by Him. He is the way in the door by which you must enter into Me, the Sea Pacific."

"The soul doesn't see itself in itself, seeking its own consolation, either spiritual or temporal. The soul has destroyed its own will and shuns no torments, but rather, enduring torments, insults, and the devil's temptations to honor Me and the salvation of souls; seeking no reward for Me or other creatures, stripped of mercenary love, simply for the praise and glory of My Holy Name, purely through love alone."

"The soul strips itself of the "old person," that is of its sensuality, and clothes itself in the "new person" through Christ Jesus, My Truth, and follows its soul meaningfully."

"Mortification of the body helps one to stay its own will, but not as an end of itself."

"In this third state, the soul is in constant peace and quiet because it destroyed its own will and has united with God the Father's will...This soul rejoices in everything that does not judge My servants or any rational creature... even if the soul sees others falling into sin but intercedes with Me, saying, 'Today, it is your turn, and tomorrow, it will be mine, unless divine grace preserves me.'"

"When an injury is done to someone else My servants endure it with compassion of the injured neighbor without murmuring against the person who caused the injury or the individual who received it because their love is not distorted but has been ordered in Me, the Eternal God."

"Never assume the right to judge the will of a person but only the will of My clemency through the Holy Spirit."

"I am the Supreme and Eternal Purity, the fire which purifies the soul, and the closer the soul is to Me, the purer it becomes. The further the soul is from Me, the more purity leaves it, which is the reason people of the world fall into inequities."

"No one can judge the secrets of the heart of a person. Sinners may frequently have good intentions, even if it externally looks like a mortal sin, seeing nothing and others but My will through holy compassion. The soul will arrive in perfect purity because it will not be scandalized, either in Me or in its neighbor. Otherwise, one may fall into contempt of its neighbor if it judges his or her will as evil, instead of My will acting on that person."

"Such contempt separates the soul from Me and prevents perfection, and in some cases, deprives a soul of grace according to the gravity of its contempt and the hatred which the soul's judgement has conceived against its neighbor."

"Everything I give or permit to happen to you, I give so that you may arrive at the end of life on earth, for that which I created you."

"The soul who remains in love of its neighbor remains always in Mine, and this remains united to Me."

"I love you inestimably and of the will of others to discern My will only and not their evil will for I am their judge, not you. Through this, you will arrive at perfection. I will tell you and show you how men should never discern by judgement but only with holy compassion."

69. ETERNAL LIFE IN THIS LIFE

"It is not yet perfect but expected perfection in immortal life, insofar as the soul begins to hunger for the honor of eternal life and for salvation—not through perfection of itself but through faith and the certitude, which the soul has of reaching the completion of the soul's being clothed in My truth. The soul has earned the reward of My love and of its neighbor. The soul is not yet perfect but expects perfection in mortal life, but not the perfection of My saints, who have died a physical death, and the soul has arrived at Me."

"The soul is blessed by the union of its holy desire toward Me, depriving itself of its will and through self-love, depriving sensual delights in consolations."

70. SAINT CATHERINE'S PRAYER FOR THE HOLY CHURCH

INTENTIONS:

"Humble servant
The whole world specifically
The Mystical Body of the Holy Church
My two parents
The Church's ministers
My family including twenty-four siblings."

SAINT CATHERINE'S PRAYER

"Since You are the acceptor of holy desires, I, Your unworthy servant, with Your grace observe Your commandments and Your doctrine to the edification of my neighbor, knowing that I love You with all my body, my mind, and my heart first and foremost through the Holy Trinity to be with you in eternal life in heaven."

71. GOD'S REPLY TO SAINT CATHERINE'S PRAYER

"Apply yourself to pray for all rational creatures, particularly My mystical body, your family, friends, and acquaintances. Be careful not to be negligent in giving them the benefit of your prayers and the example of your life, teaching them your words, correcting vice, and encouraging virtue according to your ability. My providence will never fail you and every person if they are humble and receive that which they are fit to receive."

72. PRIESTLY DIGNITY - THE EUCHARIST AND UNWORTHY COMMUNICANTS

"I have placed the ministers of the Holy Church in an excellent position with dignity."

"I have especially chosen My ministers for the sake of your salvation, so that through them, My only begotten Son may be administered to you."

"My Son is one thing with us, the Holy Spirit, proceeding from the Father and the Son, and We together form One. That is to say, I, the Eternal God, have preceded the Son and the Holy Spirit

"To the Holy Spirit is attributed fire, and to the Son wisdom, by which the wisdom of My ministers receive the light of grace so that they may administer this light to others with gratitude for the benefits received from Me by the doctrine of My Son."

"I have entrusted My ministers in the Mystical Body of the Holy Church, so that you may have life, receiving His body in food and His blood in drink."

"You received the whole Divine Essence in that most sweet sacrament concealed under the witness of the bread. The whole of God and the whole of man cannot be separated under the white mantle of the host for even if the host should be divided into a million particles, in each particle, I am present as the whole God and as the whole man."

"Each person who receives the Eucharist produces a holy desire individually to the soul's ability. The host is material bread, but the real material given to you is love for through love I have created you, and without love, you cannot live. Your being, given to you through love, has received the right through Holy Baptism, which you receive in virtue of the Blood of the Word, and no other way could you participate in this light. You would be like a candle without a wick inside."

"The holy faith which you receive by grace in baptism, united with the disposition of your soul created by Me, so filled for love, that without love, which is the soul's very food, the soul cannot live."

"Since you are created in My image and likeness and being Christians possess the light of Holy Baptism, each of you may grow in love and virtue by the help of My grace as may please you by your free will to increase in love of Me and your neighbor by using it while you have time. When time has passed you, you can no longer do so."

"The grace that you receive in the sacrament of the Eucharist is dependent on the holy desire with which you dispose yourself to receive it."

"Receive it in the state of mortal sin, not having produced true contrition and confession, and the soul does not obtain grace and is only confused with a remorseful conscience."

73. HOW BODILY SENTIMENTS ARE DECEIVED BY THE EUCHARIST BUT NOT SOULS

"Seeing the whiteness of the host and the taste of the bread are the physical phenomena of the Eucharist."

"The real significance is the divine nature united with human nature, the Body, the Soul, and the Blood of Christ—the soul united with the body and the soul united with My divine nature, not detached from Me."

"The eye of the intellect has true vision; using the pupil of holy faith should be your principal means of vision as it cannot be deceived. This is the way you should look at the Eucharist along with the palate. With a fiery desire, the soul tastes My burning charity, My ineffable love, with which I have made the soul worthy to receive the mystery of the sacrament and the graces associated with it."

74. GRACES OF THE SACRAMENT OF THE EUCHARIST FOOD OF THE ANGELS

"Graces remain after the bread has been consumed by My divine charity and the clemency of the Holy Spirit. The wisdom of My only begotten Son, by which the eyes of the intellect...know the doctrine of My truth, and together with this wisdom, you participate in My strength and power, which strengthens the soul against sensual self-love, against the devil, and against the world...being constantly united to Me."

"You are constrained and obliged to render Me love because I love you so much. Being the Supreme and Eternal Goodness, I deserve your love."

75. PRIESTLY DIGNITY DEMANDS GREATER PURITY

"I have called My ministers so that your grief at their miseries may be more intense. If they considered their dignity themselves, they would not be in the darkness of mortal sin nor defile the face of their souls."

"They are My anointed ones, so I call them My Christ's because I have given them the office of administering to you as I have appointed them earthly angels in this life."

"In all souls, I demand purity and charity, that they should love Me and their neighbor, helping souls through the ministry's prayer, but far more so from My ministers."

"Of my ministers I require:
Purity and cleanliness of heart, soul, and mind
Bodies to be instruments of the soul in perfect charity
Not to feed or wallow in a mire of filth
Not to seek great prelacies
Not be cruel to themselves or to their fellow creatures through sin
Draw souls out of the hands of the devil
Administer My sacraments of the Holy Church."

76. VIRTUES AND HOLY WORKS OF MY MINISTERS

"Peter, the prince of the apostles, who received the keys to the kingdom of heaven and others who have been placed in different ranks, administered according to their state of grace through the Holy Spirit, which they have drawn from true light but not with light alone."

"The light cannot be separated from the warmth and color of grace; therefore, a person must have the light of warmth and color of grace or none at all."

"A person in mortal sin is deprived of the life of grace, and one who's in grace has illuminated the eye of one's intellect to know Me...One's own selfishness on which account one hates it, thereby receiving the warmth of divine affection, which follows one's intellect by filling one's memory through My doctrine."

"The light, warmth, and color are united as one thing, having one power of the soul aligned to receive Me in My Name."

"Therefore, as the eye of the intellect lifts itself with the pupil of faith above sensual vision in contemplation of Me, and memory is filled with that which an aligned affection loves, the soul participates in Me with My power and the wisdom of My only begotten Son with the fiery clemency of the Holy Spirit."

"My elected ministers, anointed and placed in the Mystical Body of the Holy Church as ministers to Me for My Son, through the Eucharist with all the other sacraments following the doctrine of My truth...Which produces fruit from barren souls with the light of their science, driving away mortal sin and infidelity by the example of their holy and regular lives."

"Peter with preaching doctrine; Gregory with science and Holy Scripture; Sylvester against the infidels; Jerome,

Augustine, Thomas all extirpated error with true and perfect humility—all were martyrs, their blood, virtue, and existential faith developed by their means."

"Prelates are placed in the position of Christ's prelacy... with the light of discretion."

"Charitably correcting them with benignity with the sharpness of fire forgiving sin with the correction of penance according to the graveness of the fault."

"Cut off evildoers without contrition for mortal sin from the congregation so that other members may not be corrupted in mortal sin because the root of self-love is alive in them."

"If My ministers do see and they do not correct but allow themselves to be bound over with clattering words or with many presents, and they themselves find an excuse for the guilty ones not to be punished...Christ said: 'These are blind leaders of the blind, and if the blind lead the blind, they both fall into the ditch.'"

"They fear not to correct. He who does not desire lordship or prelacy will not fear to lose it and will correct appropriately. He whose conscience does not correct him of guilt does not fear."

"My ministers embraced voluntary poverty and sought out vileness with profound humility and cared not for scorners, villains, insults, opprobrium, pain, tormentors, or the distraction of adversarial people."

"They are truly not angels by nature but through My goodness are guardians, and therefore, they have their eye continually over those under them, inspiring in their hearts holy and good thoughts, offering them up before Me as sweet and amorous desires. Continual prayer, desire, divine words, and examples of life are offered up as well through the Mystical Body of the Holy Church."

"Through the largeness of their charity and of the hope that they had placed in My providence, they were without servile fear, either spiritual or temporal. A sign that a creature hopes in Me and not in oneself is that one does not fear with servile fear...They who hope in themselves are the ones who fear and are afraid of their own shadow and doubt lest the sky and earth fade away before them."

"The miserable, faithless, and proud ones consider not that I alone am He, who provides all things necessary for the soul and the body. My creatures hope in Me, that My providence will be measured to them. The miserable ones do not regard the fact that I am He who is and they are the ones who are not. They have received their being and every other additional grace from My goodness."

"It is true that I desire you to use your being and exercise the graces I have bestowed upon you in virtue, using your free will, which I have given you with the light of reason. I created you without your help. I will not save you without it."

"My love was and is the companion of whosoever desires it with the light of faith, hope, true patience, and long perseverance, even until death."

"In eternal life, I have placed My ministers in the greatest dignity. They receive blessing and glory in My sight because they gave the example of a holy life...They are beloved by Me because this treasure, which I placed in their hands, was not hidden through negligence or ignorance, but they recognized it to be from Me and exercised it with care and profound humility, with real and true virtues. I, for the salvation of souls, placed them at such a high standard; they never rested, putting My creatures into the Holy Church. Even out of love and hunger for souls, they gave themselves to die to get them out of the hands of the devil...They corrected them and gave them penance for their sins. They committed thorough love and endured their penance with them... They showed themselves simple with insignificant love. They knew how to be all things to all people, giving each one nourishment."

77. REVERENCE SHOULD BE PAID PRIESTS

"My ministers act on the authority and dignity that I have given them. I do not wish them to be punished by seculars because of any personal defect. Those who punish them offend Me miserably...I wish for seculars to hold them in due reverence, not for their own sake but for Mine or by a person of the authority which I have given them dignity, belonging to good and bad alike."

"You should hate the defects of those who live miserably in sin. I forbid you to appoint yourselves their judge... This is your duty according to the demands of charity, and thus, I wish you to act with regard to such badly ordered priests, who themselves with vice through their separation from My love; even though they are separated from My love, they can still bring you great treasures (sacraments), but their sins indeed should displease you and hate their sins...Pray to Me and My goodness with a garment of charity, if only they will dispose themselves to receive it and you to pray for it... It is not My will that they should be in this state; you should pray for them and not judge them, leaving their judgement to Me."

78. DEATH OF A JUST MAN VS. DEATH OF A SINNER

"So that you may have greater compassion for these poor wretches and how the peace of a just person's death is a perfection of one's soul."

"I want you to know that all sufferings which rational creatures endure depend on their will. If their will were in accordance with Mine, they would endure no suffering, not that they would not have physical or mental problems. Labor produces no suffering to a will, which gladly endures them, seeing that they are ordained by My will...People naturally fear death, but the will of a just person, perfectly aligned with God, transcend nature... through a person's conscience, intellect, and free will. One remains at peace with oneself and by the grace of Christ through the Holy Spirit."

"Such people wage war with the world, the devil, and their own sensuality through holy hatred of themselves. They die peacefully because they have vanquished during their lifetime by binding sensuality like a slave with the reign of reason, penance, and humble, continual prayer...The just person does not turn his or her head to admire past virtues because the will cannot hope in its own virtues but only in the Blood, in which the soul has found mercy."

"The devil, through the poison of sin, produces no terror or fear as it would for another who had lived wickedly in the world."

"The devil's war cannot hurt a perfect soul at the time of death. The eye of the intellect, illuminated by the pupil of holy faith, sees Me, the Infinite and Eternal Good, whom the soul hopes to obtain by grace, not as its due but by virtue of Jesus Christ, My Son...That soul arrives at the 'gates of heaven with the happiness of an angelic nature, but to a far greater degree, by ministers, who have lived like angels with a greater hunger for the salvation of souls...My ministers have a supernatural light, which these men possess over and above virtuous living through holy science, by which they know more of My truth. He who knows more, loves Me more and receives more."

"Your reward is measured according to the measure of your love. If you would ask Me whether one who has no science can attain this love, I would reply, yes, it is possible, but an individual case does not make a general law."

"A minister's conscience gives good testimony of him to Me, and I justly give him the crown of justice adorned with **pearls of virtue...** and if he has faithfully and accurately followed the doctrine of the Good Shepherd... In them, there is no poison of sin; thus there is no servile fear in them, only holy fear."

79. THE DEATH OF SINNERS IN THE HOUR OF DEATH

"How terrible and dark is the death of a sinner. The devil attacks them with great terror and darkness, including showing his face. So greatly does he freshen the sting of conscience that it gnaws at the soul horribly."

"The sinner's life was unfaithful to Me."

"Selfishness has veiled the pupil of most holy faith; therefore, the devil torments souls with infidelity to bring the soul to despair."

"As a member of the devil, sinners are disarmed without the armor of affection of charity; therefore, they don't have either supernatural light or science. The horns of their pride don't let them understand My love and mercy."

"I tell you that so great is shame and confusion unless sinners in their lives has a habit of hoping in My mercy to forgive them of sin. Religion is a great presumption of My mercy. They may error by falling into a state of despair and would arrive with the devil in eternal damnation."

"However, arriving at the extremity of death with recognition of sin, the conscience is unloaded by Holy Confession, and presumption is removed so that the soul offends Me no more and mercy remains. With this mercy, sinners are able to proceed with hope, not so that they should offend Me by means of mercy, but rather, that they should aspire to My charity by grieving for sins and perfectly requesting My mercy...If sorrow is carried out in the right way, their sorrow will procure mercy."

"One who despairs despises My mercy, making one's sin to be greater than mercy and goodness."

"Grieving for one's own loss but not the offense done to Me therefore receives eternal damnation...Had the soul grieved and repented for the offense done to Me and hoped in My mercy, the soul would have found mercy. For as I have said My mercy is greater without any comparison than any sin a creature can commit. Therefore, it greatly displeases Me that they should consider their sins to be greater."

"Despair is that sin which is pardoned neither here nor hereafter...This is the reason during their lives I use this sweet trick...With hope in My mercy, they may arrive at death, and they are not so inclined to abandon sin on account of the severe condemnation. They receive as if they had not nourished themselves with all the time and great hope in My mercy. They did nothing but offend Me miserably in a state of presumption and would not do My will, but rather, hide it under the ground of disordinate selfishness; then now it renders one the fruit of death."

"Brought up your children, enriched your relatives, throwing it away on gluttony, many silver vessels or other adornments for your house. Even spent money on harlots, when you should have lived in voluntary poverty as an obedient minister."

"Sins that are further problems for My ministers:
Pleasing creatures for the sake of gifts
That which you should not have and did
Not providing mercy
Pleasant word hiding the truth
Related to neglecting the divine office
Foul-mouthed heresy is mortal sin
That which you should have done and didn't."

"At the time of death, the evil person's conscience places virtues and sins before them, together with the virtues that person ought to have practiced, for the soul's greater shame...The evil person sees its own life was devoid of any virtue...and pain is produced with darkness of mortal sin...Not to make the soul despair, so that through perfect self-knowledge and shame of its sins but with hope, so that the soul may pay for its sins, appeasing My anger and humbly begging My mercy."

"To the just person, the appearance of the devil produces no harm or fear at the time of death...when the soul begins to see its errors, the soul's beatitudes are recognized in joy."

"Those who have passed their lives lasciviously receive both harm and fear from the appearance of the devil, not despair unless they wish it...But the condemnation of a suffering conscience."

"My ministers, for the most part, have received Me, enlightened by Holy Scriptures. The greater their obligation, the more their intolerable confusion develops for not fulfilling them...Their torments are greater than those of others, just as good men are placed in a higher degree of excellence."

"My ministers who become corrupt and suck the blood from My Holy Church are punished greater than seculars, according to their state in life, stripping properties and seizing prelacies for their own advantage through their evil lives. Seculars are found to be irreverent and disobedient to the Holy Church."

80. SAINT CATHERINES' PRAYER FOR THE HOLY CHURCH

"You have shown to all creatures so much burning love beyond common charity...You alone are charity. Whenever a creature is given charity, it would be more than that creature would ever need. You, who gives grace to us through love and not as our due."

"Adam's sin, because of his human nature, as a physician, You gave me the medicine that can cure us from our infirmity by the eye of the intellect with the light of most holy faith. You have also given grace to humanity through the Mystical Body of the Holy Church."

"Humanity learns by the dignity of Your ministers, who You have appointed us...Your anointed ones, who ought to be earthly angels in this life...So that men can better understand the sins of those who live wretched lives"

"They can, however, do harm to the world as mirrors of sin when they ought to be mirrors of virtue...so that people may wholly arise out of the infirmity of ignorance and negligence in knowing themselves and the offenses committed against You by all sorts of people.

"You have created us in Your image and likeness. Recreate them to grace in Your mercy and the Blood of Your Son, sweet Christ Jesus." Amen.

IV. OBEDIENCE
→ LIFE

HEAVEN

GRACE
VIRTUE

GRACE
+
TRUE VIRTUE

FRUIT
FLOWERS

DISCRETION

OBEDIENCE
+

BRANCHES

THE SOUL'S LOVE OF GOD

+

SOUL
(Infinite)
-Memory
-Intellect
-Free Will

Observe
MY
Commands

TRUNK
(Finite)

SOIL
Soul's Humility

FATHERS WORDS

ROOT
GOD

TREE OF LOVE AND LIFE

"The whole of one's faith is founded upon obedience."
"By faith you prove your fidelity."
"My providence, the Word, repaired the key of obedience."
"Without humility obedience dies in a soul."

IV. TREATISE OF OBEDIENCE

Sections 81-89

81. OUTLINE OF OBEDIENCE

"Obedience is found in its completeness in the sweet words of My only begotten Son."

DESTRUCTION OF OBEDIENCE

"Look at the first man, and you will see the cause which destroyed the obedience imposed on the Eternal Father was pride by Adam, which was produced by selfishness and desire to please his companion...I deprived him of the perfection of obedience, giving him instead disobedience, depriving him of the life of grace and slaying his innocence. He then fell into impurity and great misery, not only Adam but the whole human race."

"One cannot reach eternal life if one is not obedient... The door is locked...Humanity did not return to Me at its end...Therefore, the keys were placed in the hands of My Son...He said in the Holy Gospel that, 'No one could come to Me, the Father, if not by Him.'"

"Christ on earth has proclaimed that, 'You are all obliged to obey Him until death.' Whoever is outside His obedience is in a state of damnation."

"Signs of personal obedience from clear vision, which the soul saw, the Divine Essence and the Eternal Trinity, thus always looking at Me, the eternal God."

"Love cannot be alone but is accompanied by the true and loyal virtues that draw their life from the love of My only begotten Son, who possesses them all but in a different way from that which humanity does."

VIRTUES UNITED TO OBEDIENCE

"Charity is the mother of patience."
"Patience is the marrow of obedience."
"Obedience is proportionate to humility."
"Humility is the foster mother of charity."

DEVELOPMENT OF OBEDIENCE

"A soul that has charity and patience, which is the marrow of obedience, has humility. One has all or none."

"Disobedience comes from pride, which issues from selfishness and deprives the soul of humility."

"Selfishness produces disobedience, impatience, and pride, and infidelity leads to the soul's external death."

"My only begotten Son's Word caused pain to Himself in His bodily life to please Me by fulfilling the obedience imposed on Him by Me."

82. OBEDIENCE IS THE KEY WITH WHICH HEAVEN IS OPENED

"The whole of your faith is founded upon obedience. By faith, you prove your fidelity."

"You are in general by My truth to obey the commandments of the law, the chief of which is to love Me above everything and your neighbor as yourself. These commandments are bound together. They infuse as you cannot observe or transgress one without observing or transgressing both."

"If a person does not unlock the gate of heaven by means of the key of faith...that soul will never enter heaven despite its having been opened by the Word. I created you without yourselves; however, I will not save you without yourself."

"Placing your love in finite things, as foolish people do, who would follow the first man, their first father (Adam), following his example of pride, impurity, and self-love...Humanity would have been destroyed by My only begotten Son, the Word."

"He repaired humanity, no matter how much a man may have spoiled his key by his free will. By the same free will assisted by grace, a person can repair it with the same instruments that were used by My Word...You must relieve mortal sin by a holy confession, contrition of heart, satisfaction, and purpose for amendment."

"Bind this key with the cord of self-contempt and hatred of yourself for the world. Fasten it to the love of pleasing Me, your Creator."

"You have come out of the mortal servitude of your own sensuality, which destroyed your dignity. Having slain this enemy with hatred and dislike of your own pleasure, you have re-obtained your liberty."

"A soul without the cord of self-contempt is not perfectly dressed."

"Patience is united to obedience. If people suffer a little fatigue, mental or corporal with tribulation, and if it happens out of the hand of holy desire, it loosens its grasp, and those people will lose it."

"They can find it again, if they wish to while they live, and if they do not wish, they will never find it. Demonstrating impatience proves that obedience does not exist in their souls."

"A soul with obedience, born in charity and founded in faith, feels not hatred when injured. The soul will strip itself of worldly vices to find peace and quiet in the holy desire of Me."

"A soul who has formal obedience, the appointed key of heaven, finds peace and quiet. You have come out of the moral servitude of your own sensuality, which destroyed your dignity. You have slain this enemy with hatred and dislike of your own pleasure. You have obtained liberty."

83. OBEDIENCE VS. DISOBEDIENCE

"My providence, the Word, repaired the key of obedience."

"Worldly souls devoid of every virtue do the contrary and go from bad to worse, from sin to sin, from misery to misery, from darkness to darkness, and death to death until they finally reach the edge of the ditch of death, gnawed by the worm of their conscience."

"It is true that souls can obey the precepts of the law if these souls do it, having time to repent of their disobedience. It is very hard for them to do so because of their long habit of sin. Therefore, let no person trust this way of finding the key of obedience at the moment of death."

"A person should not put such trust in hope as long as that person has had a lifetime to delay repentance."

"Because the cloud of self-love and wretched pride, though they have abandoned obedience and fell into disobedience, they are impatient. Their impatience endures intolerable pain, seducing them from the way of the truth, leading them along with lies, making them slaves and friends of the devil's. Unless they invent themselves with patience, they will go to eternal torment."

"My beloved sons, obedient and observers of the law, rejoice and exult in My eternal vision in this life; they taste one supreme infinite good, and by:

Satisfaction without disgust
Riches without poverty
Peace without disturbance
Every good without evil
Safety without fear
Hunger without pain
Light without darkness."

IV. TREATISE OF OBEDIENCE

"How? By virtue of the Blood of the Lamb, whose key opens the door to heaven through obedience."

"Extinguish the hatred you have for your neighbor by abandoning injustice, murder, hatreds, rancor, detractions, murmuring, false judgements, cruelty, thefts, treacheries, disordinate pleasures, and other delights of the world."

"You will see that remaining in hatred, you injure Me by transgressing My precept, and you deprive Him of your love, whereas you have been commanded to love Me above everything else and your neighbor as yourself... Literally, you should observe it, and if you don't, you will injure your own soul, depriving it of the life of grace."

84. A SPECIAL TYPE OF OBEDIENCE IS SUPER LOVE

"Souls that exist with a true hatred of self-love develop a perfection of obedience, so that they become observers of councils in deed and in thought."

"They either place themselves under the yoke of obedience and holy religion, or without entering religion, they bind themselves to some creature, submitting their will to people, so as more expeditiously to unlock the door of heaven, not altering the fundamental principle of the virtues."

85. ADVANCEMENT OF GENERAL TO PARTICULAR OBEDIENCE BY RELIGIOUS ORDERS

"General obedience advances to the second level of obedience by sunlight as one acquires the first."

"Through most holy faith, the soul would have learned in the Blood of the humble Lamb My truth, the infallible love of which I have for a soul and its own fragility, which cannot respond to Me with due perfection. However, the soul will wander, seeking by that light in what way and place the soul's debt can be paid, retaining the soul's will."

"Enlightened in the soul's search by faith, holy religion is found through the Holy Spirit, appointed to those who wish to obtain perfection."

"The Holy Spirit, as captain of the ship, never fails in Himself through the defects of any of His religious subjects, who may transgress the rule of order. The 'Ship' itself cannot be damaged, but only the offender."

"A soul on fire with desire and a holy self-hatred is having found the soul's place by the light of faith and enters there as one dead, and if the soul is truly obedient, if the soul has perfectly observed general obedience, even if the soul is initially imperfect when entering, perfect obedience may be attained by exercising the virtue of obedience."

"Entry can be through perfection, the virtue of childhood, fear of penance, or other allurements. It depends on after entry if they exercise themselves in virtue."

"Obedience depends on perseverance until death for no true judgement can be made on a person's entrance into religion, only on the love of those rules of order provided for by his master, the Holy Spirit."

"Through divine providence, My servants might be poor, but never beggars."

"When religious orders live virtuously in true poverty at fraternal love (charity), their temporal substance never fails them. Because self-serving private possessions they held in obedience, their temporal substance failed. Had they observed the vow of poverty, each would not have taken his own and lived privately."

"Examples of poverty, Saint Benedict and Saint Francis:
True and holy poverty
Not desiring to please any creature
But only His will
Thought vile by the world
Slaying his will
Accepting insults, sufferings, and jibes."

"The humble Lamb was fastened and nailed to the cross by love so that by a singular grace, there appeared in His body the very wounds of His truth."

"Showing that in the vessel of His body that which was in the love of His soul, so He prepared the way."

"The principle foundation of religious orders is charity."

ORDER OF SAINT DOMINIC

"Father Dominic, My beloved Son ordered it most perfectly, wishing that his sons:

Should apply themselves only to My honor, praise and glory for salvation of souls
The light of science as their foundation

They shouldn't hold any possessions either in community
or privately to extirpate errors
A light which I gave the world by means of Mary, who
gave him his habit
He chose poverty so not to care for temporal things
Vow of continence for every man in thought or deed
Prevent pride to develop obedience
Humility in proportion to obedience

"The pillars of obedience, continence, and true poverty
via pain of mortal sin if not obeyed. Not the desire for
the death of a sinner, but rather, converted to live."

"St. Paul, whose eyes illuminated that the darkness of
error was dissipated by their glance."

"St. Thomas (Aquinas), his gentle eye of intellect at the
truth, dissipated clouds of heresy."

"St. Peter at his death wrote the credo on the ground, a
martyr and virgin, who by his blood gave light among
the darkness of many heresies. His life was nothing but
prayer, preaching, hearing confessions, announcing the
truth, and spreading faith without fear."

"Everything an obedient religious does is a source of
merit to themselves...Those people have abandoned
themselves with self-hatred to the arms of the order
and the superior. Those people remain strong and firm,
having lost all weakness and fear, having destroyed
their own will, from which comes all feebleness and
disordinate fear."

"The obedient religious speaks words of peace all of their
lives and at death, receives that which was promised to

them at death by their superior—that is, eternal life, the vision of peace, and supreme eternal tranquility."

"Like a vessel dipped into the sea does not comprehend the whole sea but only the quantity it contains, the sea alone contains itself. I, the sea Pacific, and He, who alone contains Himself and can comprehend Myself and rejoice in the good which I have in Myself that I share with you according to the measure of each. I do not leave you empty but fill you, giving you perfect beatitude."

86. THE OBEDIENT AND DISOBEDIENT RELIGIOUS ORDERS

"Obedience through light of holy faith, by which the soul must slay its selfishness with the hatred of every sensual passion...developed by patience and humility. Without humility, obedience dies in a soul."

"The key of obedience of a minister's order will open a panel of the door of heaven."

"Men of an order cast from themselves the land of the riches, and of their own will observe the vow of voluntary poverty, refusing to possess anything. For they will see by the light of faith to what ruin they would come if they transgressed obedience and the vow of poverty which they promised to keep."

"The vow of continence if transgressed lives in their own pleasure, going on to close intimacy, not like a religious but like nobles without watching or prayer...They fall into mental and physical impurity. Sometimes, from shame, they have nothing physically but mentally with bad habits and disordinate greediness. They don't pray to preserve purity of mind."

"He is to pass through the door and not leave the order but walk the narrow path of obedience to his superior."

"The perfectly obedient puts miseries above himself and his own sensuality by living faith, placing selfishness as servant of his soul to drive out the enemy of selfishness, producing peace and quiet with the enemies of the soul exiled."

"The enemies are selfishness, producing pride, the enemy of humility and charity. Impatience is the enemy of patience, disobedience of true obedience, and infidelity of faith; presumption and self-confidence are not in accord with true hope, which the soul should have in Me. Injustice cannot be conformed to justice nor imprudence to prudence nor intemperance to temperance nor transgressions of the commandments of the order to perfect servants of them nor the wicked conversation of those who live in sin to the good conversation of my servants...Anger against benevolence, cruelty against kindness, wrath against benign hatred of virtue versus love of virtue, impurity versus chastity, negligence versus ignorance versus self-knowledge, and sloth against watchfulness and continued prayer."

"The obedient man is patience, patience being the sister of obedience."

"Is he disgusted and angry at performing humble duties that might produce mockeries? No, for he has conceived love for self-contempt and self-hatred."

"His conversation is with those who truly fear Me, and if he should converse with those who are separated from My will, it is not in order to conform himself to their sins but to draw them out of their misery."

"He endeavors to convert religious and secular by his words, by prayer, and by every means by which he can draw them out of the darkness of mortal sin."

"The conversation of a truly just, obedient man is good and perfect, whether they be with just men or with sinners, through his rightly ordered love and the breadth of his charity."

"Through an illusion of the devil...He fixes the eye of his intellect on Me and sees with the light of faith that I am his helper."

"When mental prayer is impossible, he recites vocal prayer or busies himself with some corporal exercises so that by these means, he may avoid idleness."

"An obedient man deprives himself today of what he needs, rather than thinking of his corporeal needs for tomorrow, most importantly thinking only of the kingdom of heaven."

"Blows inflicted on him by his superiors in the order but calling him humbly turn him without anger, hatred, or rancor but with meekness and benevolence."

"He observes the vows of poverty, true obedience, and continence, having abandoned the heights of pride, and bows his head to obedience through humility."

"Calling a child, He said, 'Allow the little ones to come to Me, for such is the Kingdom of Heaven to be. Whoever will not humble himself like this child, that is keeping his childlike condition, shall not enter the Kingdom of Heaven. He who humbles himself will be exalted and he who exalts himself will be humbled.'"

87. THE OBEDIENT PERSON RECEIVES 1:100X AND ETERNAL LIFE

"Peter's demand: 'Master, we have left everything for love's sake and have followed you. What will you give us?' Jesus said, 'As hundredfold for one and you shall possess eternal life. That is in return for the gift for his own will be 100 times. The obedient will obtain eternal life by charity alone. It is not by faith that they taste eternal life, nor by hope. Charity alone enters and possesses Me, the soul's possessor. They possess wonderful and hardy joy. There is no sadness in charity, but the joy of it makes the heart large and generous, not narrow or double, because they have received this hundredfold from Me.'"

"The soul who possesses charity will never fall into depression or the affliction of sadness or jars with obedience but remain obedient ."

88. THE DISOBEDIENT PERSON'S MISERIES

"A wicked disobedient man dwells in a religious order in so much pain to himself and others that in his life he experiences the seriousness of hell! He always remains in sadness and confusion of mind, tormented by the sting of conscience with hatred of his order, superior, and in support of himself...a masquerader, who does not see that he is in danger of death, at which time he will have no remedy."

"Because a religious has to preach My doctrine, he may do so in polished terms, but not as one who should feed souls with the seed of My Word. This deprives him of the light of grace, giving him eternal death

"The result of a contrary is not a religious man but an incarnate devil...The intellect deludes itself by self-love, which is fixed on pleasing itself on things of the world through the devil's deceit."

89. GOD REWARDS MERIT OF LABOR BY LOVE

"Holy obedience is a state of inebriation with love and obedience to the Word, losing oneself of one's own opinion and knowledge by pleasing Me through grace and love by the light of holy faith."

"Obedience is serving one's neighbor...promptly and pleasing to Me."

Example: "Jesus's vineyard parable"

IV. DISOBEDIENCE
→ DEATH

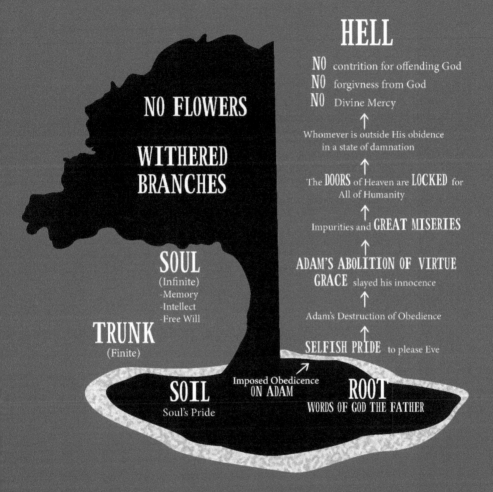

HELL

NO contrition for offending God
NO forgivness from God
NO Divine Mercy

↑

Whomever is outside His obidence
in a state of damnation

↑

The DOORS of Heaven are LOCKED for
All of Humanity

↑

Impurities and GREAT MISERIES

↑

ADAM'S ABOLITION OF VIRTUE
GRACE slayed his innocence

↑

Adam's Destruction of Obedience

↑

SELFISH PRIDE to please Eve

NO FLOWERS

**WITHERED
BRANCHES**

SOUL
(Infinite)
-Memory
-Intellect
-Free Will

TRUNK
(Finite)

SOIL
Soul's Pride

Imposed Obedience
ON ADAM

ROOT
WORDS OF GOD THE FATHER

TREE OF DEATH

"Christ on earth has proclaimed that you are obliged
to obey Him until death."

"Let no person trust the way of finding the key
of obedience at the moment of death."

V. CONCLUSION

Sections 90-91

90. DIALOGUE SUMMARY

CHARITY - THE DIALOGUE'S OBJECT: "To increase the fire of My love in your soul."

FAITH - "Through the light of faith acquired through your desire to obtain knowledge of My truth and understanding yourself."

HOPE - "Requesting of Me to provide mercy for the world."

MYSTICAL BODY - "You prayed for the Mystical Body of the Holy Church, that I would remove darkness and persecution from it, punishing its inequities at your desire in your person."

SIN - "No penalty inflicted in finite time on earth can satisfy a sin committed against Me, the Infinite Good, unless it is united with the desire of the soul and contrition of the heart."

MERCY - "I wish to do this by mercy to the world, proving to you that mercy is My special attribute, and through mercy and the inestimable love which I had for mankind, I sent to the earth the Word, My only begotten Son, so you might understand things quite clearly. An example is the analogy of the bridge, reaching from earth to heaven through the union of My divinity with your human nature."

BRIDGE - "It reaches from heaven to earth through the union of My divinity with your human nature...It is built on three steps. That is, with the three powers of the soul: (1) feet (2) through the side and (3) the mouth. And the three states by which the soul arrives at the excellence of unitive love: (1) imperfect (2) perfect (3) most perfect. Each state means cutting away imperfection and reaching perfection...so that the soul may avoid the hidden delusions of the devil and of spiritual self-love."

CLEMENCY - "My clemency delivers: (1) in this life (2) at death in mortal sin without hope (3) the last of the last and universal judgement. Suffering of the damned and glory of the blessed, when all shall have resumed their bodies given by Me."

REVERENCE - "The reverence I wish seculars would hold toward My ministers should not be diminished because of the sins they commit and the virtue of those who live like angels. The excellence of the sacraments. All tears issued from the fountain of the heart and pointed out their causes and their four states, including the fifth, which germinates death."

DIVINE PROVIDENCE - "I have explained how everything is made from divine providence...Permitting everything that happens to you for your good in order that you may be sanctified in Me and My truth be fulfilled in you. The truth is that I created you in order to possess eternal life, and manifest this with the Blood of My only begotten Son, the Word."

OBEDIENCE - "I promise to speak of the perfection of obedience and the imperfection of disobedience and how obedience may be perfected. Obedience is the universal key of religious orders and those of the world...The peace and the war of the world. Death comes into the world by disobedience like Adam's sin and of life by the World of My only begotten Son."

SELF-KNOWLEDGE - "I urge you and My other servants to grieve. By your grief and humble prayer, I will do mercy to the world. Die to things of this world and hasten along this way of truth so as not to be taken prisoner if you move slowly. I demand this of you now more than at first because now I have manifested to you My truth in the cell of self-knowledge, which is a doctrine of truth founded on the living stone, sweet Jesus Christ, clothed in light which scatters darkness."

91. SAINT CATHERINE'S FINAL PRAYER

"My God grant that my memory may be capable of retaining your benefits...and I give the blood of my body out of love, together with the key of obedience, so that I may unlock the door of heaven."

"You are my Creator; I am the work of Your hands. What more could You have given me through a new creation, the Blood of Your Son?"

"I see through faith that my soul is alive, and in this light, receive you, the true light, that I have acquired wisdom in the wisdom of the Word...through faith, I am strong, constant, and persevering in the light of faith."

"I hope, suffer me not to faint by the way...Hold me with the hand of Your love so that I may see myself as Your creature, represented in You and Yourself in me through You, which You made of Your God-head with our humanity."

"Through faith, many wonderful things have been declared to me, explaining to me the path of perfection...I could not see You as You are without the gift of holy faith and the doctrine of truth...Because I did not see with the glorious light of holy faith, the cloud of self-love darkening the eye of my intellect."

"Through my soul's intellect and the light of holy faith and the truth excellence of obedience, with love and ecstatic desire, giving thanks our Eternal Father. You have not despised me ... because of my infirmities."

"You are eternal Purity, who are the infinite, have overlooked that I am finite and sinful... through Your clemency, You have forgiven Me.

"I have found Your charity and love of my neighbor. May that same charity constrain You to illuminate the eye of my intellect with the light of faith so that I may know and understand the truth which You have manifested to me."

"I hope suffer not to faint along the way...Hold me with the hand of Your love so that I may see myself as Your creature represented in You and Yourself in me through You made of Your God-head with our humanity."

"O, eternal Trinity, deep-Sea, the deeper I enter the more I find the more I seek...Melt at once the cloud of my body and to give my life for the greater honor and glory in praise of Your Holy Name."

"You have been willing to condescend to my need and to all creatures the need of introspection, having first given to ask the question...You replied to it and satisfied it, penetrating me with a ray of grace, to go in that light; I may be forever grateful to You, my God. Amen!"

REFERENCES

1. Algar Thorold, *The Dialogue of the Seraphic Virgin,* (London: K. Paul et al.1896)

2. TAN CLASSICS, *The Dialogue of Saint Catherine of Siena,* (Benedict Press, 2010)

3. Etienne Cartier, *The life of Saint Catherine of Siena,* by Blessed Raymond of Capua, Translated by The Ladies of the Sacred Heart (Philadelphia, Pa: P.F. Cunningham, 1860) @ catholicsaints.info/alphabetical-list (Catherine of Siena, e-book, 2020)

4. Pope Benedict XVI, (General Audience 24 November, 2010) @ catholicsaints.info/alphabetical-list (Catherine-of Siena, 2021)

5. Author Unknown, *The Dauntless Virgin of Siena,* (Australian Catholic Society, 1955) @ catholicsaints.info/alphabetical-list (Catherine of Siena, e-book, 2021)

6. Suzanne Noffke OP, *Classics of Western Spirituality, The Dialogue (*NJ, USA: Paulist Press, 2002)

7. Lodovico Ferretti, *Saint Catherine of Siena,* (Italy, Stampato da Cantagalli, 2004)

8. Augusta T. Drane, *History of Saint Catherine of Siena* V2, (London,: Burns and Oates, 1882) @catholicsaints.info/ alphabetical-list (Catherine of Siena, e-book 2021)

9. Patricia S. Churchland, *Conscience, The Origins of Moral Intuition, (*New York/London: Norton & Co. 2019)

ACKNOWLEDGEMENTS

It would have been impossible for this editor to have conceived the format developed for this Dialogue without the scholarly works of Blessed Raymond of Capua, Etienne Cartier, Augusta Drane, and Algar Thorold. My prayers of thanksgiving to our Creator for the development of these treatises for humanity, along with the bloggers at catholicsaints. info/alphabetical-list for their e-books.

Thanks, especially to my wife Eunice, who tolerated the COVID-19 lockdown with her own ingenuity to provide me the incentive to use Brain HQ.com, a regenerative computer program to bring an eighty-year-old cerebral cortex back into its' early seventies. My granddaughter Kaitlyn, a talented graphic artist, under the tutelage of her mother Suzanne, my daughter, and son-in-law, Brooks Lewis, was always pulling the loose ends together and teaching me the value of a computer-savvy family.

For all of the staff, both administrative and service personnel, at Saint Paul's Plaza, my assisted living community, and especially my new friends at the Plaza that provided the environment and extra minutes on a daily basis to keep me focused on this book. I am especially grateful.

Last, but not least, the talent and perseverance of the staff at Xulon Publishing who guided this novice author with expertise to develop satisfaction in a new career. Thanks again!

APPENDIX

TOPIC OUTLINE REFERENCE

Sections 1-91

GOD'S LOVE

1. For Humanity - 1,9,13,16,44,45,46,51,58,62,63,66,68,84,91

2. Divine Mercy - 13,14,18,20,28,29,90
3. Salvation of Souls - 6,11,20,38,48,58,72,79
4. Fire of My Love in Your Soul - 4,45,90
5. The World's Three Corrections - 27
6. Infinite Service - 63

7. Tree of Love and Life - 10, IMAGE #2

HUMANITY'S PAIN

8. Suffering in Earthly Life - 3,5,35,54,58

9. Purgatory - 4,33,42,55

10. Final Judgement - 20,30,31,32,33

11. Keys to Heaven - 18,63,81,82,83

12. Errant Priests - 77,78

13. Perfect Love for Salvation - 4,7,44,45,46,47,49.51,52,53,64

14. Contrition - 13,50,53

15. Humanity's physical and Mental Pain - 35.58

16. Soul at Death of the Body -56,70,79

17. Pain of the Damned - 32

18. Just vs. Damned Souls - 32,33,78

HUMANITY'S PAIN RELIEF

19. Peace and Happiness - 78

20.Tools for Eternal Life or Death - 38,40,41,69,78,79

21. Humanity's Soul - Definition in Preface 10,12,13,14,31,37,38, 40,54,56,58,62,63,66,68,74

22. Christ's Bridge - 15,16,17,18,19,20,37,40,43,47

23. Humanity's Tears - 60,61,62,63,64,67

24. Striving for Perfection - 66,67,68,69,84

HOLY SCRIPTURE REAFFIRMED

25. Trinity Documentation - 20,26,46,72,

26. Eucharistic Transubstantiation - 50,58,72,73,74

27. Hatred - 83

28. Original Sin and Adam - 4,6,13,14,33,81

29, God in a Unitive State with a Soul - 10,31,37,42,54,58,59

30. Christ Crucified- 26,30,49,53,59

31. Praise to God - 54,55,63

GOOD vs. EVIL

32. The Light of Reason - 66

33. Virtue vs. Vice - 6,7,8,22,23,24,66,78,79

34. Law of Perversity - 66

35. Creators Commands - 36,37,40

36. Love vs. Self-love - 24,34,44,48,49,62,68,74

37. Self-love is Selfishness Produced by Sensuality - 6,7

I think that I shall never see
A poem as lovely as a tree

A tree whose hungry mouth is prest
Against the sweet earth's flowing breast;

A tree that looks at God all day,
And lifts her leafy arms to pray;

A tree that may in summer wear
A nest of robins in her hair;

Upon whose bosom snow has lain;
Who intimately lives with rain.

Poems are made by fools like me,
But only God can make a tree.

A. JOYCE KILMER
1886-1918
American Poet

ABOUT THE AUTHOR

Raymond Anthony Hurm on June 25,1939 was born to Tony and Clotilda Vesper-Hurm in Covington Kentucky, and raised between Newport and Fort Thomas, Kentucky. He graduated from the Covington Latin School in 1955, Xavier University, Cincinnati, Ohio in 1959 with a BS in Biology and a M.D. in 1966 from Loyola University Chicago, Illinois. The next three years involved a general surgery residency at the Good Samaritan Hospital in Cincinnati, Ohio. He was commissioned in the USAF as a partially trained surgeon, with the rank of captain, serving in the medical corps with a stint in Vietnam assigned to the US Army. Following that time of service, he completed a residency in urology at the University of Wisconsin, Madison, in1973, obtaining AUA board certification in both adult and pediatric urology. He developed Urology Specialists Ltd. in Phoenix, Arizona, in 1974 where he remained in private practice for forty- one years. He retired in 2014 to Coronado California, where he owned a home for twenty- five years. In 2019 a move to an assisted living facility in Chula Vista, CA. with his wife, Eunice, of fifty-seven years, provided an opportunity to renew his verve in philosophy and theology, where at Xavier he acquired minor degrees in both studies. Hobbies of golf, tennis and sailing all slowed down in 2020 on a new career of authorship, for which he had been trained in earlier educational endeavors, as well as in his urology career.

CPSIA information can be obtained
at www.ICGtesting.com
Printed in the USA
LVHW070050260422
717021LV00006B/9